Cana Academy®

HISTORY
Forgotten and Remembered

Andrew J. Zwerneman

Published by
Cana Academy®
www.canaacademy.org

Cover image: Replica of compass rose in Pedro Reinel's nautical chart of 1504, photographed by Joaquim Alves Gaspar, uploaded to English Wikimedia Commons by user Fibonacci on May 24, 2007. Used under https://creativecommons.org/licenses/by/2.5/deed.en.

To Rich Preuss,
my good friend
who always remember
what the Lord has
given us.
Andrew
6/11/2021

for
Jeannette

Contents

Introduction: Finding Common Ground

History, it seems to me, is the most useful key we have to open the mysteries of the human predicament.

—Donald Kagan

The claim Professor Kagan makes is a bold one. It appears near the end of his 2005 Jefferson Lecture, "In Defense of History" where, having explored the contemporary state of the humanities and the society they are meant to serve, he warns that we have lost our "moral bearings." By taking a "turn to history," Kagan hopes we might recover them.[1] One may wonder if any human source could meet so great a challenge. At the same time, the proposed turn to history reminds us that unless we are to acquiesce to the loss, we must seek our bearings somewhere. This book is an invitation to make that turn—to give Kagan's key a try.

The Challenges of Teaching History

It serves another, more practical purpose as well. As it turns out, leading students in the study of history poses fairly

[1] Donald Kagan, "In Defense of History," Jefferson Lecture, National Endowment for the Humanities, 2005, https://www.neh.gov/about/awards/jefferson-lecture/donald-kagan-biography. Kagan is Sterling Professor Emeritus of Classics and History at Yale University and one of the world's preeminent scholars of Greek antiquity.

unique challenges. I hear about them from teachers all over the country. Typically, their concerns take the form of these questions:

How do I choose between competing concepts of history? Is history just one thing after another? Is it more or less a catalogue of facts? Does history repeat itself? Is it progressing somehow?

What makes historians select the events that make it into their works?

You hear someone warn, "History will judge us," or, "This person is on the wrong side of history." Does history act somehow as a force or agent?

Are history and memory distinct?

What is the relationship between history and experiences that are not strictly matters of facticity, even transcendent experiences?

It is not that these teachers do not know historical content. Rather, they want to know more and gain greater clarity about how to think historically, and they want their students to develop the best historical habits of mind.

Additionally, teachers regularly voice concerns that, as a field of study, history seems caught up in the current cultural turmoil our society faces and is moving along the same intellectual trends that are largely responsible for the general decline of the humanities. Under this concern, they ask these questions:

Some histories seem to be written more as calls to action than as studies or sources of understanding. How do we stay objective and, at the same time, allow history to shape our students' vision and responsibility?

Some historians describe the history of America and the West as a story of exploitation or oppression. What can we say in the face of such criticism that basically dismisses our culture as corrupt?

In fact, there is a growing approach to history in American schools that disparages America and the West. The general emphasis in that approach is on events having to do with class, race, and gender exploitation. Of those three, the central concern regarding America has to do with slavery and racism. Because that concern greatly shapes how American history is interpreted in our culture today, there is some significant space devoted to addressing it in the chapters below.

Finally, the question of how we study history is related directly to how we think about our humanity and the sources that gave us the language and vision with which to articulate who we are. That challenge raises this question:

My students, colleagues, and I are from various backgrounds. Is there an approach to history we can all share?

There are other related questions that emerge, mostly having to do with what a history discussion looks like, how to develop great discussion questions, how to construct an effective lecture, and what texts and documents to read. The foundational questions, however, are the most important ones to answer. Good answers to them will free teachers to map out their plans for readings, discussions, projects, and lectures.

Of all the questions laid out above, the toughest one to answer is the question that brings us face-to-face with the challenge of a common culture: *Is there an approach to history we can all share?* I believe there is, and I offer here one that transcends our divisions. It is what I call a liberal approach to history.

A Liberal Approach to History

By liberal, I intend its root meaning: free, as in persons who are genuinely free—free from undue external constraints and free from within, as in intellectually, morally, and spiritually free. That internal kind of freedom is the goal of education, and it really is a goal, not a given. We are born with free will, but we are not born free in the higher sense. We must be educated to freedom. To be free in this sense is to know the truth, to examine our thought and practice, and to seek ever greater understanding. To be free means to govern ourselves as individuals and together and to meet our shared responsibilities by pursuing ends or purposes that are noble and lasting, reflective of our dignity and of the common good. Finally, freedom means generously giving ourselves to others, even sacrificially. A liberal education is an education to freedom. It guides us to the truth of things within and beyond ourselves, to noble purposes, and, above all, to others.

With that concept of a liberal education in mind, how might we approach history as a field of study? First of all, the liberal approach to history is observational. Our study of the past is driven by wonder and the desire to know, to see the past for what it is. It is directed toward understanding. We observe the past by looking back and seeing it as distinct from the present and, at the same time, as forming who we are now and how we came to be.

Humans learn history by observing everything we can of past events; gathering knowledge and seeking understanding through the fullest study we can achieve regarding those events; avoiding all reductions of history to less than what it is; and deepening and improving our comprehension by ever expanding examination. Through the study of history, we learn about ourselves by looking beyond ourselves to those who preceded us.

Eventually, history shapes how we embrace our responsibility for one another, as do all the humanities in their various ways. However, the study of history is not, as it is often presented, primarily intended to produce action. Rather, the study of history is primarily intended to cultivate habits of the mind: wonder, inquiry, discovery, knowledge, and understanding, each with the past as its object. Again, first and foremost, history is observational.

Secondly, the liberal approach to history is sympathetic, not judgmental. By judgmental, I do not mean evaluative. I mean judgment in the sense of moralism. In this respect, to approach the past in judgment of others is to forget the condition we all share; it is one way that we forget ourselves. Sympathy, by contrast, allows public memory to collect our shared human condition across time. The root meaning of sympathy is to feel what others feel, especially their suffering. The broader meaning of sympathy is to share an affinity for others and for the full range of human experience. It presumes a common ground: the human condition, human nature, a shared past, and the hope for a future together. Sympathy embraces our capacity for transcendence, creativity, and all genuine loves. Under the impulse of sympathy, recollection extends to our predecessors, attends to their likeness in the living, and sustains our attachment to those yet to be born. In sympathy, we allow others to work on us through memory; we receive them as members of a community of persons across time. Sympathy attunes us to the poverty of our existence, that is, our limitations as individuals and our reliance on others. At the same time, it gathers in our memory and holds what is good, what creates and sustains, and what gives us hope.

Sympathy recognizes human sufferings as well, the kinds we all endure and the ones imposed by some on others. Memory holds such impositions with regret; and, as painful as it is to recall those failings, they must be retold as part of our story if for no other reason than we ought to feel the suffering of others as a matter of our common humanity. However, because of our affinity for the full breadth of the human condition, history is not, as it is often reduced to, chiefly the recollection of grievances. Rather, the primacy in our shared experience lies with what is good in our existence: the life we have, which makes all improvement possible, its origins and developments, and the inherited culture that situates us in the world.

If understanding is well established by the study of history, and if the goodness of our existence is held sympathetically in our public memory, then our shared responsibility emerges chiefly as a matter of preserving and improving the order of things. For, even when something is clearly opposed to human good—as injustice is to justice, oppression to freedom, or hatred to love—it is the good that measures it and provides meaning. It is the good that provides the foundation for creativity, improvement, and hope. Only something good can transform human suffering. Memory, then, rests on the broader, more inclusive understanding of sympathy as affinity for all things genuinely human, as the feeling that undergirds our interdependence and mutual responsibility, and as the shared confidence in the goodness and continuity of our existence as a society across the past, present, and future.

History is, on the one hand, the formal study of the past and is expressed in either academic or popular narratives. On the other hand, as a common way of thinking, history is expressed at all levels of culture. The historian approaches the past knowing that culture is already full of recollective expressions such as national holidays, liturgies, and cemeteries, just to name a few, where each one is, in part, an expression of recollection. Each gives evidence that remembering the past is part of who we are. In other words, as a formal study or as public memory, history is integral both to our understanding of what it means to be human and to our life together in society. In either expression, history is observational and sympathetic.

Glimpsing Our Future in the Past

Our culture is at a crossroads concerning our past. We have lost significant confidence regarding history as an academic study and as an everyday way of thought. As with the humanities in general, the study of history is in decline. So are the common cultural habits of mind regarding our past. In both senses, history is in crisis. As a society, we are increasingly divided from our past, which is a significant part of why we are increasingly divided from one another. To put it another way: There is a real sense in which history has been forgotten; and, having forgotten our past, we have forgotten ourselves.

As a history teacher and as a coach and mentor to fellow history teachers, I cannot avoid the relevant foundational questions. The reflections here are a personal effort to come to grips with the crisis that impacts what and how we teach. The hope is that my answers will help my fellow teachers surmount the crisis as well.

As with most difficult objects of study, one way to grasp history more clearly is to approach it by way of an image. In this case, it might help to have a past event or two brought alive through the senses. With that in mind, let us turn to a master of images, Seamus Heaney, arguably the greatest poet in the English language in the last half century. Most relevant to this exercise, Heaney is a poet and essayist who approaches the past observationally and sympathetically.

In his seminal poem, "Digging," for instance, Heaney captures the primacy of the past and the attention that it warrants here in the present. He achieves this through a recollection wherein he reconstructs events involving his forebears farming the fields of the Heaney homeland in Northern Ireland. There in the distant past, his father sinks a spade into potato drills, his grandfather goes "down to the good turf" and cuts into a peat bog. Heaney recalls his own presence there by their sides as they work the land. However, the details of the poem give Heaney the boy a very minor role; instead, the memory is formed chiefly by the fathers who came before him and by the land they worked. Their images, each one in turn, provide a unity across generations. Their greatness, detailed in the physicality and the precision with which they open up the ground, seems to define the adult Heaney as different from his fathers, he with his pen, they with their spades.

The remembrance proves revelatory, at once an interruption of his present life, a measurement and an illumination of his given place in the world, and a vision of his calling as a poet. In other words, through memory, Heaney allows his fathers to work on him. As the poem winds down, Heaney's reflection develops into a definitive response:

The cold smell of potato mould, the squelch and slap
Of soggy peat, the curt cuts of an edge
Through living roots awaken in my head.
But I've no spade to follow men like them.

Between my finger and my thumb
The squat pen rests.
I'll dig with it.[2]

As any student of modern history knows, the land of Heaney and his forebears has not been all life and unity. In fact, shortly after he came into his own as a poet in the 1960s, Northern Ireland exploded from within, a deadly convergence of British domination, Christian sectarianism, unbending claims of minority and majority rights, and terrorism. In his 1995 Nobel Prize address, the great poet shifts genres, adopting the historian's role and recollecting those difficult events for his audience. Note here his emphasis on *change*:[3]

> The external reality and inner dynamic of happenings in Northern Ireland between 1968 and 1974 were symptomatic of change, violent change admittedly, but change nevertheless, and for the minority living there, change had been long overdue. It should have come early, as the result of the ferment of protest on the streets in the late sixties, but that was not to be

---

[2] Seamus Heaney, "Digging," in *Opened Ground: Selected Poems*, 1966-1996 (New York: Farrar, Straus and Giroux, 1998), 3.

[3] Heaney, "Crediting Poetry: The Nobel Lecture," in *Opened Ground*, 420-421.

> and the eggs of danger which were always incubating got hatched out very quickly.

Part of him, what he called the "Christian moralist," recoiled at the Provisional IRA's (Irish Republican Army) violence; the "'mere Irish'" in him judged the ruthless British Army. He knew that "if life in Northern Ireland were ever really to flourish, change had to take place." Yet, the Provisional IRA, the chief catalyst for change, was destroying the "trust upon which new possibilities" must be founded. The division that marked Northern Ireland triggered "violence from below" against "violence from above." For decades, the life and spirit that could have formed the foundations of genuine cultural renewal were wasted. Northern Ireland needed an exodus, a path to a better existence. In this story, Heaney glimpsed the way forward:

> One of the most harrowing moments in the whole history of the harrowing of the heart in Northern Ireland came when a minibus full of workers being driven home one January evening in 1976 was held up by armed and masked men and the occupants of the van ordered at gunpoint to line up at the side of the road. Then one of the masked executioners said to them, "Any Catholics among you, step out here." As it happened, this particular group, with one exception, were all Protestants, so the presumption must have been that the masked men were Protestant paramilitaries about to carry out a tit-for-tat sectarian killing of the Catholic as the odd man out, the one who

> would have been presumed to be in sympathy with the IRA and all its actions. It was a terrible moment for him, caught between dread and witness, but he did make a motion to step forward. Then, the story goes, in that split second of decision, and in the relative cover of the winter evening darkness, he felt the hand of the Protestant worker next to him take his hand and squeeze it in a signal that said no, don't move, we'll not betray you, nobody need know what faith or party you belong to. All in vain, however, for the man stepped out of the line; but instead of finding a gun at his temple, he was thrown backward and away as the gunmen opened fire on those remaining in the line, for these were not Protestant terrorists, but members, presumably, of the Provisional IRA.[4]

Heaney might well have focused his account on the terrorists, the story's oppressors. As a master rhetorician, he could have wielded his words like bullets from a gun and fired off a moral hail against the workers' mortal enemy. Along the way, Heaney might have turned his pen on the British who, in the first place, bore no small responsibility for the general disorder that marked Northern Ireland. Instead, he focuses our gaze elsewhere in the event to what is most memorable, meaningful, and hopeful:

> The birth of the future we desire is surely in the contraction which that terrified Catholic felt on the

[4] Heaney, "Crediting Poetry," 421-422.

> roadside when another hand gripped his hand, not in the gunfire that followed, so absolute and so desolate, if also so much a part of the music of what happens.[5]

It is not that Heaney hides from evil; nor is it that he cannot or does not distinguish between oppressor and oppressed. Rather, his evaluative distinctions are illuminated by a defining glimpse that allows him to complete the account, something far more difficult to comprehend than the lines drawn between opponents, something hidden as the hands of the workers were in the twilight. In the bond briefly formed between the Protestant who died and the Catholic who lived, the one offering life to the other, the other choosing "witness" over life only to discover his false saviors as murderers and his true savior as victim, Heaney glimpses their common humanity. Over and against the division between Protestant and Catholic, their quiet solidarity stands out as the greater response, more significant than the lines drawn between the actors in the event. That is the truth revealed in the event because, while the division between them and between their attackers and themselves offers neither life nor hope, what they hold in common does.

Through memory, Heaney lets the two workers work on him. Imaginatively, he writes them large—the measure of Northern Ireland's life and hope. Through his story-telling, at once observational and sympathetic, Heaney represents every Irishman and every human as the life of any one of us is made possible when "contraction" precedes "birth."

---

[5] Heaney, "Crediting Poetry," 421-422.

The bit of history he tells has its force in the very specific details he collects of this otherwise isolated event. The day is a day not unlike others. The year is 1976, a year like any other year, full of countless events not remembered as this one event is now. The event happens along a nondescript road. Still, it all takes place in Northern Ireland. In that place and at that moment in the history of that land, a handful of countrymen, akin yet so opposed to one another, meet up and play out their choices amidst the strained state of things. The prevailing disorder in which they act, formed between "violence from below" and "violence from above," is uncreative and lifeless. It signals a costly forgetfulness concerning a life together.

Yet, two men, normally defined by what divides them, stand firm on what they have in common, and each, in his own way, gives what he has for the other. Because of that singular event, and because it was told in public so that Heaney had absorbed it, and, finally, because Heaney retells the story with an observant, sympathetic eye, we now remember the two workers, hand in hand. The truth of their common humanity rediscovered in that fateful moment, the higher purpose each one expressed under the threat of violence, and the sacrificial generosity each exhibited, are, taken all together, an occasion to remember their freedom, and ours.

I. Unrepeatable Events

The distinction between historian and poet . . . really consists in this, that the one describes the thing that has been, and the other a kind of thing that might be.

—Aristotle

As a form of Western literature, history has a storied record, extending back to Herodotus' *Histories* and Thucydides' *History of the Peloponnesian War*. Each of those writers thought that past events are repeated: They thought, in other words, that history is cyclical. Thucydides emphasized the constancy of human nature as a foundation for expecting that past events "will happen again in the same or in a similar way."[6] Neither writer thought there is a goal to history, a purpose or end that transcends historical events and in which those events will culminate. While their cyclical approach to history did not become the prevailing concept in the West but eventually gave way to one that is purposeful, the histories of Herodotus and Thucydides are still read as classic works, and their conviction that we learn from the past in important ways has been a bedrock conviction for our culture.

---

[6] Thucydides, *History of the Peloponnesian War*, trans. Rex Warner (New York: Penguin, 1954), 48.

Aristotle's Limited View of History

However, as a field of study, history's place in liberal education had an uncertain start. Aristotle, the father of the liberal arts, gives history very limited reference—and even then, most famously, internal to his study of poetics. There, he says just three things: History is about the past. It is about what actually was, as opposed to what could be, which is what he finds in epics and dramas. And, in regard to past events, we can speak of singulars but not universals.[7] In other words, at best, we can record the facts of events. In that sense, history is a rough equivalent to a patient's medical record—a set of facts concerning the individual's health and illness, but not a biographical account that penetrates either the personality of the patient or the meaning of the patient's life. For Aristotle, there seems to be little or no importance to human history as narrative. That kind of fuller account of human action is left to the imitative art of poetry as he finds in epics and dramas.

In his analysis of rhetoric, he remarks how helpful it is to know examples of past events since they are indicative of what will happen in the future.[8] Aristotle gathered a remarkable range of constitutions on which he based his comparative political study.[9] His *Metaphysics* includes some cultural history—specifically, how the arts and sciences developed.[10] In other words, Aristotle observes the kinds of things a historian works up in reconstructing past events into a

---

[7] Aristotle, *Poetics*, 1451b1-10.

[8] Aristotle, *Rhetoric*, 1394a5-10.

[9] Aristotle, *Nicomachean Ethics*, 1181b.15-20; *Politics*, II-IV.

[10] Aristotle, *Metaphysics*, 981b14–24.

narrative. Still, he neither uses them narratively nor develops an account of history as a science, as he did with politics, or an art, as he did with rhetoric.

As part of his practical science of ethics and politics, Aristotle has some important things to say about memory, which one might expect he would connect to history as the remembrance of the past. Internal to the *Nicomachean Ethics*, Aristotle comes very close to doing that. Specifically, in his discussion of friendship, he accounts for memory's vital part in political order.[11] In his *Politics*, he also notes that a polity develops from the family; thus, he treats the organic growth of human relationships from smaller to greater in a way similar to how botanists or zoologists once treated developments in natural history.[12] Ultimately, however, Aristotle does not contemplate a historical society in action—no full consideration, for example, of the Greek wars with Persia or the long and ultimately self-destructive Athenian war with Sparta, nor careful biographical analyses of major Athenian figures such as Solon or Pericles.

For Aristotle, because historical events are singulars, no two of them are the same in the flow of time; and time seems to be like Heraclitus' famed river, constantly flowing, constantly changing. Given the constant motion of time, each event, then, is a unique moment; every past event is an unrepeatable change. At best we can record events as changes as a doctor or nurse records the pulse rates and temperature of a

---

[11] Aristotle, *Nicomachean Ethics*, 1166a.25.
[12] Aristotle, *Politics*, I, 1.1252b.9-1253a.1-2.

patient or as a chronicler records sequential change without reading it in its full context or relating it as a story. Change is evident elsewhere in reality, and Aristotle notes change as an important factor in his works on physics and metaphysics.[13] However, he seems never to have developed history as a science, and the singularity of what has happened in the past is never collected in narrative form.

I am going to return to the matter of memory later and address how we might think about the relationship between history and order in a way similar to how Aristotle relates individual memory and order. For now, we need to look more closely through the crack in the door that Aristotle leaves—the one regarding history as such. Whatever else it might be, we can all agree with him that history is about the past. On the surface, that does not sound like much on which to develop a practical vision of history. If we are going to get further along in our understanding of the past than merely as a time-flow of unrepeatable events, we will need more than what Aristotle has to offer on history.

If, on the other hand, Aristotle is right concerning the singularity or unrepeatability of events, then we will also need more than what our first historians, Herodotus and Thucydides, offered. There is no doubt that past events are familiar to us and that they illuminate later ones. Even Aristotle seems to agree with his predecessors on that point. We can as well. Still, the concept of history as cyclical has not prevailed in the West. In either case, following Aristotle on the pastness of

[13] Aristotle, *Physics*, VI; *Metaphysics*, V.2.

history or Herodotus and Thucydides on the familiarity and illuminative power of past events, what else can we say about history? What else do we need to establish in order to situate history in a liberal education?

II. The Enduring Past

[B]y and large, "history" is interested in the eruptions of the extraordinary into the flow of the regular.

—Wilfred M. McClay

We have noted that time is a flow and that the past is forever gone. We have also noted that the past is unrepeatable. Or, to put it another way, each event is a unique change; and, in the flow of time, change is constant. What else can we do other than note the singularity of events? A good place for further insight is in the nature of time. Let us start with a two-pronged observation about time as the flow in which events happen:

> (1) Time is a necessary condition for history: that is, every event happens in time.
> (2) Time is an insufficient criterion for an event to be remembered.

What does that mean for our understanding of events? For one thing, of all that is in the past, few events make their way into our historical thinking. Countless incidents have happened in the past. Only a relatively small number of events are selected as part of our public memory or as objects of formal study. The fact that the Greeks won at Marathon in 490 BC, or the British at Trafalgar in 1805 AD, does not account for why those battles are among the relatively few heralded by

Greek and British peoples and examined in history books. After all, countless events happened in 490 BC and 1805 AD. That these two battles are included in works of history is not adequately explained by the date of their occurrence. Time simply is not sufficient for events to penetrate our public memory nor to warrant the attention of historians. Other criteria clearly are needed.

Events In and Beyond Their Times

For another thing, the significance of past events is not restricted to the time in which they happened. None of us, for example, were alive at the moment of the Battle of Gettysburg in the summer of 1863 nor when Lincoln delivered his iconic address later that year. Yet, long after those events, Lincoln's words have haunted us. In the case of Martin Luther King, Jr., we clearly see evidence of the lasting power of Lincoln's words. On the occasion of his "I Have a Dream" speech in 1963, not only did King speak from the steps of the Lincoln Memorial, which in itself was evocative of events a century earlier, he measured the very moment of the occasion in rhetorical terms similar to the words used in Lincoln's opening line at Gettysburg. Speaking in 1863, the late president hearkened to the American Founding with the measurement "Four score and seven years ago," which directed his audience to the year 1776 and the signing of the Declaration of Independence. King situated his audience with "Five score years ago," a measurement that directed everyone back to

1863, the year of Lincoln's Gettysburg Address and the year his Emancipation Proclamation went into effect.

Lincoln's audience was not alive in 1776, nor was King's in 1863. In neither case, then, were the events a matter of individual memory. Still, against the seemingly insuperable distance of a past that no longer existed, the events of 1776 and 1863 were summoned with great force; they were remembered as sources that could give America a foundation and direction in the midst of a national crisis. In each case, the nation was divided and in need of a recollection of what could unite us. Each speaker drew from our past and developed his speech from there. Such is the potential power of history as our public memory: It brings time forward from the distant past to the present and directs our vision to a yet more meaningful future as Lincoln and King did.

History as Change

That past events endure is one thing; why they endure is another. There is, in other words, the matter of history's selectivity. University of Oklahoma historian Wilfred M. McClay offers a good answer to why events endure. He begins with this general observation about the past: One way to understand history as a field of study is as the "study of change in time."[14] By "change," he means how a society moves across the past to the present. There are two senses of movement

[14] Wilfred M. McClay, *Land of Hope: An Invitation to the Great American Story* (New York: Encounter Books, 2019), xiii.

in this regard: A society, the largest of which is a civilization, moves chronologically from one time to later ones. That kind of change is clearly discernible as the sequence of years with their corresponding figures, places, and events. Greece warred with Persia, for example, from 499 (Ionian Revolt) to 449 BC (peace was struck). Central Persian figures were Darius (first invasion) and Xerxes (second invasion); the central Greeks were Miltiades (Marathon), Leonidas (Thermopylae), and Themistocles (Salamis). And while most of Greece, including Athens, fell to the Persians, the small alliance of Greeks eventually defeated the imperial invaders.

A society also moves qualitatively. Herodotus saw the Persian Wars, and Thucydides the Peloponnesian War, as events around which to understand the past as a whole. Each war burst onto the field of history, overcame each previous event with its greater significance, and held out to future readers changes worth their attention:

> May the great and wonderful deeds—some brought forth by the Hellenes, others by the barbarians—not go unsung; as well as the causes that led them to make war on each other.[15]
>
> —Herodotus on the Persian Wars

> [I] wrote the history of the war fought between Athens and Sparta...in belief that it was going to be a

[15] Herodotus, *The Landmark Herodotus, The Histories*, ed. Robert B. Strassler, trans. Andrea L. Purvis (New York: Pantheon, 2007), 3.

> great war and more worth writing about than any of those which had taken place in the past.[16]
>
> —Thucydides on the Peloponnesian War

In recounting the Greek victory over Persia, Herodotus heralds the height of Athenian greatness. Thucydides, by contrast, traces Athens' steep decline, one from which it never recovered, a loss made more poignant by the fact that the Syracusans who defeated Athens in the fateful Sicilian expedition, like the Athenians, were democrats.[17] Polybius measured the Punic Wars in a similar way to Herodotus and Thucydides. He interpreted Rome's imperial growth as the defining feature of history, so much so that history's goal was the completion of that Roman expansion.[18]

As the Greek examples indicate, qualitative change does not always mean change for the good. We can agree that some changes are movements toward order—the introduction of limitations on absolute monarchy established by the Magna Carta, for example, or the restoration of international relations between America and Europe through the Marshall Plan after World War II. Others are recognizable as movements toward disorder—the Reign of Terror during the French Revolution, for instance, or the rise of twentieth-century dictatorships.

---

[16] Thucydides, *History of the Peloponnesian War*, 35.

[17] Victor Davis Hanson, *A War Like No Other: How the Athenians and Spartans Fought the Peloponnesian War* (New York: Random House, 2005), 311.

[18] Karl Löwith, *Meaning in History: The Theological Implications of the Philosophy of History* (Chicago: University of Chicago Press, 1949), 7-8.

From this qualitative way of thinking, the founding of America is an important change in history: the genesis of a new country and one that developed into one of the major players on the world stage. America's history is punctuated by events of varying, sometimes opposing, qualitative force: the settlement of colonies mostly by British subjects, the slave trade, the ratification of our constitution, civil war, the expansion west, the numerous conflicts with and ultimate displacement of natives, great waves of immigration, the explosion of industry, energy and technology, the World Wars, the Cold War, the sexual revolution, the Civil Rights movement, and the victorious race to the moon, just to name a few.

"Eruptions of the Extraordinary"

Why, in turn, are all these singular events remembered? They are what McClay calls the "eruptions of the extraordinary into the regular."[19] In other words, changes most worth examining are momentous, culture-changing events; and, again, some changes are toward order, some toward disorder.

There is no significant sense in which extraordinary events are repeated, even when events have something familiar about them. We recognize a modern ruler as a tyrant, for example, but we would not rightly say that Hitler and Stalin are merely repeats of Caligula or Ivan the Terrible or that they are exactly identical to each other. Each is distinct, and each caused distinctive disorder in his respective country.

---

[19] McClay, *Land of Hope*, xiii.

Unrepeatability applies to all human action and to all categories of human events. It is also a reminder of a bedrock feature of human nature, namely free will. Because each human has free will, no two humans carry out their actions in exactly the same way. Each human event, then, is in some measure unique and unrepeatable; each is a distinct change. Finally, because of free will, the outcomes of human events are not inevitable. To put this another way: Past events happened the way they did, not the way they had to happen.

This indeterminacy has broader implications for our understanding of history. For one thing, of all beings in the world, we alone are capable of choosing and acting in ways that either fulfill our ends and purposes or fail to do so. For another, the "age" or "era" in which we locate an event is at most descriptive; it determines neither the direction of a change—toward order or disorder—nor its level of significance. The Golden Age of ancient Athens, for example, did not make Athenian democracy, victory at Salamis and Marathon, or Aeschylean tragedy what they were. Rather, the name for the age reflects such events and draws on them for its descriptive accuracy.

At the same time, the singularity and unrepeatability of events does not mean that events are altogether independent from each other. History is the study of change in time, and one change always succeeds prior ones and precedes its successors; at no time is a change, even an extraordinary one, strictly an isolated event. There is always the flow of time in which an event occurs. More importantly, history is the study of change in the existence of a whole—the whole society or the entire civilization in which an event occurs. When Julius Caesar crossed the Rubicon, it was an extraordinary event in the extraordinary history of Rome. The Rubicon River, however, was just that, a river. As a river, it held no historical significance on its own. Crossing it meant nothing if the crossing was isolated from its context. The historical significance of Julius Caesar's crossing the Rubicon is only understandable in the context of Rome as a whole. In this case, the boundaries set around the city of Rome placed restrictions on generals and their armies from approaching the empire's capital. A violation of one such restriction portended civil war.

Of course, the flow of change in time, punctuated by the extraordinary, need not end in the past. It can and, in some discernible ways, does continue today. Think of the influence of Greek and Roman culture on America. There is, for example, classical architecture as a model for America's most important buildings. Note the Corinthian columns that adorn the outside of the Supreme Court building and the Ionic its interior courtroom; or note the building's general design derived from ancient Roman temples. Roman roads, for another example, were engineered to advance the empire; thus, they were prerequisites for the development of the West, as were the ways of thinking inherited from Hellenic Greece.[20] Cicero's classical natural law writings would shape the

[20] Bruno Snell, *The Discovery of the Mind: The Greek Origins of European Thought* (Tacoma: Angelico, 2013), v.

political thought of the American founders.[21] Classical statuary, informed by Hellenic sensibilities regarding form, would extend its influence into the Italian Renaissance; later, the Renaissance sculptures of Michaelangelo would influence the modern sculptors Rodin and Meštrović, whose works adorn public places in America.[22] Roman legal and executive structures were among the sources that shaped how the founders conceived of American political order.[23]

The influence of ancient Greece and Rome has not ceased, even as those cultures have. The eruptive events of their storied past were extraordinary then; they remain extraordinary as civilizational sources. What I am saying of ancient Greece and Rome I could say of ancient Israel, which gave us an entire field of symbols and practices that still fuel our culture: the ubiquitous cross, for example, a remembrance of Christ's death, or the prevalence of Christmas in public and private festivities. I could say something similar of Britain too, with its enduring contributions of common law, the English language, and its culture of adventure and discovery. All these are among the extraordinary events that interrupted the ordinary flow of things and that continue to influence the ordinary flow of our existence in America.

---

[21] A.J. Beitzinger, *A History of American Political Thought* (New York: Harper and Row, 1972), 4.

[22] For example, Rodin's *Burghers of Calais* stands in Washington, D.C.'s Hirshhorn Sculpture Garden, Philadelphia's Rodin Museum, and the campus of Stanford University; Meštrović's works mark the Croation embassy to the United States, the gates of Grant Park in Chicago, and the campus of the University of Notre Dame.

[23] Forrest McDonald, *The American Presidency: An Intellectual History* (Lawrence: University of Kansas Press, 1994), 77-88.

History as a Source of Practical Wisdom

One final thought regarding the impact of the extraordinary on our present existence: History, as we have considered it so far, is a necessary field of study by which we understand the connection between the past and the present. On another level, history is also necessary for the cultivation of society. In other words, we draw upon the past in order to preserve and advance our culture. As McClay puts it, without history as the collection of our public memories,

> we cannot do the most human of things: we cannot learn, use language, pass on knowledge, raise children, establish rules of conduct, engage in science, or dwell harmoniously in a society. Without [history] we cannot govern ourselves.[24]

In other words, there is a practical wisdom that history makes possible, a combination of experience and understanding that sustains us. History helps us see our society and maintain it the way that Lincoln's invocation of the founding and King's of Lincoln illuminated America at the respective crossroads of 1863 and 1963. The language America used to move away from slavery and segregation was a language deeply embedded in our history and in the history of the West. The 13th, 14th, and 15th amendments enacted in the 1860s and the Civil Rights Act and Voting Rights Act, enacted in 1964 and 1965 respectively, reflected that historical language and forged further into the law of the land our understanding of

---

[24] McClay, *Land of Hope*, xii.

and commitment to freedom and equality. Our history is undeniably flawed. At the same time, that same history made it possible for us to move beyond those flaws and improve the political order with the later amendments and acts.

III. Observing Others

The task of the historian is to understand the peoples of the past better than they understand themselves.

—Herbert Butterfield

The bulk of what humans learn about ourselves is beyond ourselves. We learn what it means to exist and to thrive as persons primarily by observing others. This is true in young children who learn and develop by looking into the faces of their parents and siblings each day, by being held by them and spoken to in words quickly familiar but only gradually understood and used in response. This is true also in literature and art where material is arranged in ways that illuminate and move us. How do we learn observationally in the field of history?

Events in Context

Harvard's Bernard Bailyn, who for decades was the leading scholar of early America, describes the field of history in terms of its attentive, creative approach to the details of the past:

> History . . . is the reconstruction of past events, circumstances, and people based on the belief that the past is not only distant from us but also different.

> Historians look for differences in the past and for how those differences changed and evolved to create the world we know, which contains, however deeply buried, the residues of those past worlds.[25]

In other words, history operates at once by a disciplined adherence to fact and out of a reverence for distinction. The adherence to fact lies in the disciplined work of history, the "reconstruction." The facts themselves lie in "events, circumstances, and people," the details that afford us the material out of which to work up a story of the past. The reverence for distinction is evident in the sustained belief that the past is different from the present and that it is formative of "the world we know."

Bailyn reminds us of something that may, on the surface, seem obvious but is increasingly neglected in the study of history: "The past is a different world, and we seek to understand it as it actually was."[26] In other words, in studying history, what we seek primarily is that which makes the past different. The key to that search is a determined focus on context. Only when we observe historical events in their context do we sufficiently grasp them. This means we should refrain from "telescoping and foreshortening" the past, which means to avoid defining it strictly in terms of the present and neglecting its difference.[27] Rather, we should

---

[25] Bernard Bailyn, *Sometimes an Art: Nine Essays on History* (New York: Alfred A. Knopf, 2015), 14.

[26] Bailyn, *Sometimes an Art*, 22.

[27] Bernard Bailyn, *Education in the Forming of American Society: Needs and Opportunities for Study* (Chapel Hill: University of North Carolina Press, 1960), 9.

follow the priorities of history as a discipline: History collects the facts of an event first, grasps them in the full context in which they occurred, and allows what is distinctive or different about the past to come into clear focus. Only then can the past's more immediate relationship with the present emerge.

Here is an example of what Bailyn means. It is not historical, he maintains, to study education in early America as if it "was simply the present writ small."[28] In the colonial era, there were few formal schools at all, and the distinction between public and private schools was generally non-existent. Families took primary responsibility for educating their children. Education was intertwined with vocational training, largely on self-sustaining family farms. Furthermore, family life was tightly connected to church communities. All of these factors shaped how colonial Americans understood civic life. That distinctive portrait of early American spirit is what Bailyn means by context and by what is distinctive in the past; for one thing, that spirit bears a significantly different look from today.[29] To rightly understand the role of education in the history of American society, one would start with that past, understand it in its full context, and trace the changes, sometimes significant, that brought us to the present.

We could note something similar regarding the intellectual foundations of America. It is not uncommon for interpreters of America to explain our current political culture by reading it as a direct result of the liberalism that shaped

---

[28] Bailyn, *Education in the Forming of American Society*, 11.
[29] Bailyn, *Education in the Forming of American Society*, 15-49.

the founding, especially the political theory of John Locke.[30] However, the context in which the founders contemplated the new republic was complex and various. They read more history than they did political theory.[31] Montesquieu, the comparativist, not Locke, was the most oft-quoted theorist at the Constitutional Convention.[32] Their religion was pervasively Christian.[33] They bore a profound sense of community, forged partly by Puritan sensibilities.[34] The meaning of key concepts, such as "common sense," was formed by the Scottish Enlightenment.[35] As mentioned earlier, the natural law thinking of Cicero was in the air since his writings were central to every founder's education.[36] Each of the founders who studied law was steeped in the writings of William Blackstone and thereby his historical analysis of the British common law, and that tradition well preceded Locke.[37]

Given this set of historical influences, it would be questionable to narrow one's scope to Locke as the main or lone key to inter-

---

[30] Ryan T. Anderson, "Debating Liberalism," *Public Discourse*, The Witherspoon Institute, July 26, 2020, https://www.thepublicdiscourse.com/featured/debating-liberalism-at-public-discourse/. Anderson provides a summary of the debate, housed by *Public Discourse,* over the influence of liberalism on America from the Founding through contemporary American culture. The debate focuses in no small measure on the writings of John Locke.

[31] McDonald, *The American Presidency*, 67-97.

[32] Donald S. Lutz, "The Relative Influence of European Writers on Late Eighteenth-Century American Political Thought," *The American Political Science Review* 78, no. 1 (1984): 189-97, doi: 10.2307/1961257.

[33] Mark A. Noll, *A History of Christianity in the United States and Canada* (Grand Rapids: Eerdmans, 1992), 119-126.

[34] Edmund Sears Morgan, *The Puritan Family: Religion and Domestic Relations in Seventeenth-Century New England* (New York: Harper & Row, 1966), 1-12, 17-28; Gordon S. Wood, *The American Revolution: A History* (New York: Modern Library, 2002), 129.

[35] Beitzinger, *A History of American Political Thought*, 235, 238.

[36] Beitzinger, *A History of American Political Thought*, 4-5, 146.

[37] McDonald, *The American Presidency*, 27-35.

preting America's founding. All of the examples cited above indicate that there was much more going on at the time, shaping the founders' thought and forming early American culture, than Locke's writings or even liberalism in general. Context matters. Any interpretation of the founding would rightly take the fuller context of the founding into consideration.

At the same time, we cannot help but observe that the individual liberty that Locke emphasizes resonates with all kinds of Americans: in the colonists who sought to claim their rights as heirs to British liberty; in the slaves and the displaced natives who longed for the freedom once reserved for whites; for immigrants of every background who sought and continue to seek opportunity in America; for the millions of individuals who risked or lost their lives by defending the country; and for common Americans who find basic meaning in providing products and services through their labor. Those historical examples speak of an individual freedom that, through common longing, public belief, and shared responsibility, transcends autonomous individualism. As a matter of reading our history in context, we need to take careful measure of those experiences as formative of the founding, of subsequent changes, and of their observable residues in American society today, all formative in ways that are more aptly described as unifying than divisive.

IV. Others Working On Us

Each human being lives in the society of other human beings; that society was there when he was born and will continue after he dies; he comes into and goes out of it, and, while in it, must acknowledge the company of others like himself as a given and a norm.

—Gerhart Niemeyer

Bailyn never loses hold of the emphasis on observation that marks history as a field of study. His method is to construct a synthesis of observable details that is comprehensive and that can be demonstrated to be true among competing syntheses. The comprehension he expects of history is that the full set of relevant, observable details be included in an account. That a historian's account can be demonstrated as true implies that it is chiefly an occasion to observe, compare, and understand. As a field of study, history is not mainly a call to action; by situating events in their context, history primarily affords us an occasion to comprehend historical reality. Its power of persuasion lies in its appeal to evidence, synthesis, and comparison. In other words, history appeals to reason. The proper study of history does provide a foundation for the maintenance and development of our shared culture. However, that foundation and the intellectual freedom afforded us by the study of history are first and foremost matters of understanding.

At the same time, Bailyn recognizes that the past is present to us in ways that go beyond what is strictly rational. We work on the past, reconstruct it, and carefully trace its influence on the present. Yet, the past seems to work on us in our memory. While he never deviates from the historian's work of reconstructing the past, Bailyn notes that we are also on the receiving end of our encounter. Memory is not the "reconstruction of what happened"; instead, "[i]t is the spontaneous, unquestioned experience of the past."[38] Where history preserves a critical distance from the past, "memory's relation to the past is" sometimes "an embrace," sometimes "troubling." It is both "emotional" and a "moral vicarious experience."[39]

For the sake of clarity and for the sake of preserving history from any confusion with what it is not, Bailyn draws moderately sharp distinctions between history as the objective study of the past and memory as the more subjective experience of the same. The one works on the past, the other is receptive of the past. History is "intellectual," memory is "emotional." History preserves a distance from what is observed. Memory is completely present to us; it is within us, "absolute, not tentative or distant."[40] History allows us to observe the past, first from a distance, then through the formative changes that happened subsequently, and finally into the past's residues in the present. In memory, we receive the past as if it presented

[38] Bailyn, *Sometimes an Art*, 15.
[39] Bailyn, *Sometimes an Art*, 16.
[40] Bailyn, *Sometimes an Art*, 15.

itself to us. In other words, memory makes the past more personal and, therefore, more meaningful.

To make his point as clearly as possible, Bailyn applies his two concepts to contemporary advancements in the study of the slave trade in America's past. Regarding history and the distance it intrinsically preserves:

> There is obviously a history of the Atlantic slave trade and the African diaspora, and the new database and these highly professional papers [of contemporary research] have greatly improved that story. The now publicly available online database will be a permanent source for the future enrichment of our critical, contextual understanding of that long-gone phenomenon.[41]

Regarding the memory of the slave trade:

> But the memory of the slave trade is not distant; it cannot be reduced to an alien context; and it is not a critical, rational reconstruction. It is for us, in this society, a living and immediate, if vicarious, moral experience. It is buried in our consciousness and shapes our view of the world. Its sites, its symbols, its clues lie all about us... It is evoked in novels and films that are less history than memory. It is what troubles us so deeply about Jefferson and Monticello. It lies barely

[41] Bailyn, *Sometimes an Art*, 16.

> below the surface in every discussion of race relations in public policy.[42]

Yet, the distinction between history and memory is not how Bailyn leaves the matter. Each is a necessary means of understanding the past. In other words, they converge in a shared purpose: "We cannot afford to lose or diminish either [history or memory] if we are to understand who we are and how we got to be the way we are."[43]

History is more bound to time, to the past, as an object of study. Because of its intellectual distance, history is more objective, and because it is removed from the past as from the perspective of an observer, it can inform the more subjective memory. Memory, in turn, is more timeless. We call up the past to the present and experience it now as meaningful, affectively, somewhere between moral poles, between "an embrace" and "troubling." As such, that experience sustains our desire to know the past through history as a field of study, and it fuels our desire to know ourselves, not just the distant, different, changing past.

Case Study: Observing and Remembering Vietnam

I first grasped at some level the connection between history and memory as an undergraduate at the University of Notre Dame in the spring semester of 1980. At that time, the uni-

---

[42] Bailyn, *Sometimes an Art*, 16.
[43] Bailyn, *Sometimes an Art*, 17.

versity offered its first course in the history of the Vietnam War. Because of the unusually large number of attendees, the professor, the late Vincent P. DeSantis, presented his lectures in one of the largest venues on campus, the library auditorium. Just a handful of years after the last Americans left Vietnam, our young minds were burdened with questions: *Why did we get into Vietnam in the first place? How did America, the most powerful country in the world, lose the war? How did we lose for the first time?* The room was well divided politically, but it did not really matter what allegiances we held; the historical questions and their implications for how we understood ourselves as a society were important to each and all of us.

It was generally a surprise to learn of the machinations of the American presidency—not just Nixon, a common target, but Kennedy and Johnson as well. The surprise mounted as we studied how Congress, which held the purse strings, had never forced the matter to a declaration of war and, by failing to do so, seems to have weakened the constitutional order; that the Tet Offensive, the most familiar of all the battles, was not a loss but a victory for the American side, albeit costly—Vietcong and North Vietnamese casualties are estimated at nearly 40,000, American at 1,100, South Vietnamese at 2,300;[44] and that American forces never lost a major battle in the war. Finally, many of us learned for the first time how the press, viewed positively by most Americans at the time, had manipulated their coverage of the war.

---

[44] George C. Herring, *America's Longest War: The United States and Vietnam*, 1950-1975 (Hoboken: Wiley & Sons, 1979), 188.

Previously unexamined assumptions fell quickly beneath the persuasive force of the now illuminated historical events, reconstructed for us by the professor and in the scholarly work through which he guided us. Our estimation of American forces, their leadership, our political leaders, and the national culture all shifted as the events of the war came into greater focus and as our knowledge of the war supplanted our prior views. The foundations for entering the war were weaker than we had realized, the carnage wreaked by the communists in Vietnam was more devastating than we had imagined, and the military successes far greater than previously understood. The spirit of the 1960s was something all of us had known to some degree, although we were just grade-school children at the time; that spirit's role in America's engagement in Vietnam came into sharper relief.

The admixture of residual national doubt and mounting desire to recover national confidence that characterized America in the late 1970s became clearer as well. In other words, our grasp of the not so distant past and its meaning for the immediate present strengthened. The Carter election in 1976, for example, made greater sense, as would the Reagan election just a few months after the course, once we understood better what the war and its loss meant as key factors in the country's direction. America had clearly found itself widely dispersed between affective poles. The division in our society would grow in ways we did not fully anticipate then, and it flows even today from cracks in the cultural dam that developed and widened during the Vietnam War.

History students in 1980 were at a real disadvantage going into a course on that war. Both because the formal history of the war was barely developed and because the public had been misled by the government and the media, we simply could not understand what had happened in Vietnam over the previous decades. We sensed but could not measure that the changes effected by the war had altered the soul of America.

Fortunately, our history professor operated according to the observational priorities of his field. In those lectures, he gathered facts and reconstructed events as a narrative of the war. His narrative was born from sympathy for the actors in those events and for the students who inherited the impact of the drama. In that dual approach, he modeled for us how to think historically. As his students, the events of the war came into greater clarity as our own observational powers grew. On the other hand, the memory of the war now worked on us differently than it had prior to the course. That course on the Vietnam War afforded us an opportunity to think better in both ways.

Factual places and persons are the necessary conditions for events in history; they also work on us through memory. To reconstruct and to remember them are necessary to a common purpose and to understand "who we are and how we got to be the way we are."[45] Because of its relation to memory, history lies between fact and meaning.

---

[45] Bailyn, *Sometimes an Art*, 17.

V. Meaning Remembered

[I]t is impossible to understand the past unless we understand the things for which the men of the past cared for most.

—Christopher Dawson

While we can talk about the meaning of a story because we can read it in its entirety, we cannot rightly speak of the meaning *of* history since the story of all human existence is not yet over. At most we can speak of meaning *in* history. At the same time, fiction and history share an important structural feature in common. In either case, the meaning we can find lies inside: inside the details crafted into the story by a writer, in the one case, inside the memory of a society expressed in their culture, on the other.

Meaning Inside History

Take, for example, an American flag adorning a family home on Memorial Day or the Fourth of July, or a cross, for another instance, worn around a believer's neck or marking the spot where a loved one died. The symbols are directly related to concrete places, persons and past events, and their meaning is conveyed through the arrangement of details in the representation. The stars and stripes on the flag represent, respectively, the fifty states today and the original thirteen colonies that won America's independence and established the country two-and-a-half centuries ago. The shape of the cross, and the corpus when included, are details that represent the historical event of Jesus' death just outside of Jerusalem two millennia ago. In each of these cases, meaning is grounded in historical events, represented in details that remind us of those events, and collected in memory as matters of thought and feeling, understanding and love.

We know that meaning can change. For example, between the generation that won World War II and the generation that came of age in the 1960s, Americans' attachment to their country declined and became less reverent, more cynical, and increasingly regretful. Even how America remembers some of its fallen soldiers changed, as evidenced in the National Vietnam War Memorial. The monument wall is situated partly beneath the earth's surface like Emily Dickinson's sinking corniced tombs.[46] The names of the fallen are etched into black granite panels, which at their greatest height rest at ten feet, at the lowest, eight inches above ground, a design evocative of an open but healing wound. The arrangement of the wall, sunken, narrowing, and dark, moves the viewer to remember the dead soldiers as victims and as heroes. In the long, descending arms of the memorial wall, the rest of the country, especially the soldiers who returned from the war, are enfolded as those who are still healing. No other American war memorial draws Americans into such a reflection by its arrangement. At the same time, the memory of no

[46] Emily Dickinson, #479, also known by its first two lines, "Because I could not stop for death, He kindly stopped for me."

other American war is understood so strongly as a wound that needs to heal.

By contrast, World War II still retains its power to stir admiration and confidence among Americans, even though it is decades older than Vietnam. We see this in the fairly recent expansions of the National World War II Museum in New Orleans and the National Museum of the Pacific War in Fredericksburg, Texas, and in the enduring popularity of films and series based on the war, like *Saving Private Ryan* and *Band of Brothers*, each unabashedly celebrating American valor and sacrifice. The personal sacrifice that makes a war effort the common man's writ large is captured well by an observation made by Steven Spielberg in the documentary, *Five Came Back*, an account of Hollywood directors who served the nation's cause by documenting events leading up to, during, and after the war. What united the five directors and impelled them to forego careers and, in some cases, risk their lives, was their shared conviction regarding the war and what was at stake. World War II, Spielberg notes, was unprecedented as an occasion for unity of purpose: "I think everybody could see that Western Civilization was at stake, and they needed to fight or die."[47] While the five men represented a range of political viewpoints, they all found meaning in the common cause of winning the war and preserving the culture.

[47] *Five Came Back*, episode 3, "The Price of Victory," directed by Laurent Bouzereau, aired March 31, 2017, https://www.netflix.com/title/80049928.

Work, Courage, and Love

Meaning for humans has mostly to do with the core motivations that hold our lives together and sustain them. Of everything that motivates humans, three, arguably, emerge as most prominent: work, courage, and love.[48] Broadly speaking, work is what we do creatively: how we shape our lives and impact the world around us; how we foster our existence with others; and how we situate ourselves in the world through culture. Courage is the measure of our response to difficulties, which every life has. Love is the measure of our personal response to others and how we give our lives to them, even sacrificially.

Regarding work, someone might ask, *Why do I work?* The response might be, *I took the job to support my family*, or, *To serve others*. Someone else might say, *To make something beautiful*. Yet another might respond, *Nothing is more important than being a parent*, or, *This is more than a job; it's my calling*. Each of these responses is an example of an individual finding work meaningful and purposeful.

Under courage, one might ask, *How do I respond to life's difficulties?* One might respond, *I served my country, and I'd do it again in a flash*, or another, *My wife faced my sickness without complaining. Now, it's my turn to be her lifeline*. Another might respond, *I know the racial barriers are real. There is a lot of old pain and deep distrust. But we're neighbors; we have to make this work, even if the odds are against us*. Any one of

[48] Viktor Frankl, *Man's Search for Meaning* (Boston: Beacon, 2017), 110.

these is an example of a meaningful response to life's challenges.

Finally, there is love. Everyone loves something; more importantly, everyone needs to love someone and be loved. Individuals usually hold multiple loves. These are the kinds of questions we ask of our love: *What do I love? Whom do I love? Which of my loves makes all the others fall into place?* One might answer, *I've been married to her for thirty years. Best decision I ever made.* Another might respond, *Everything I do is for my kids.* Yet another, *It has not been easy, given the scandals that hit the church, but not a day goes by where I don't thank God for my calling.* Another might respond, *I never knew what it meant to love until she forgave me.* Finally, one might say, *I know, I know, there is no money in teaching. I keep teaching because I love my students.*

Note that all of the questions and answers have to do with concrete human action in time; in other words, what is meaningful is not ultimately abstract. Furthermore, none of the accounts of meaning are possible without the passage of time. Finally, along with the continuity of our existence, what is meaningful about the past is collected in our memories. In fact, another name for memory is recollection.

History as Public Memory

That the past is present to us through memory is true for an individual and for a society. For an individual person, memory gathers what a life is about. It holds one's loves and regrets, and, from the beginning to the present, it collects events from the past that constitute that individual's story and self-understanding.

History is the chief recollection of a society's past. As public memory, it collects what we know of ourselves as a society plus the continuity of our existence across time: past events, the changes that created the world we know, and the residues of the past found in the present. These things, however, are more than observable; they are meaningful because they are collected in and through our public memory.

This is true even though a society exists in ways only similar to the way an individual exists. An individual human being is a completely unified subject. When we observe someone, we really can see the whole person in action. This is not so with a society; we cannot behold its entirety. Individual members die. Generations fade into the past. New members are not yet born. Historical existence, then, is not equivalent to personal existence.

Still, to varying degrees, the culture we hold in common affords us shared experiences and a shared memory: national elections; public spectacle in liturgy, sports matches, parades, and festivals; widely broadcasted events on radio or television; commonly read works; language, manners, and customs; distinctive architecture for shared purposes. Thus, while the likeness between public and personal memory is limited, the fields of meaning are similar.

Work, Courage, and Love in America

Meaning for a society rests largely in the same three categories that matter most for individual persons. In America, for example, we recall the herculean *work* in American transportation, agriculture, energy, industry, and the construction of great works—the Transcontinental Railroad, the Brooklyn Bridge, and the Hoover Dam, for instance. We settled vast territories of wilderness and developed a staggering network of roads, lines of communication, and commerce. Work in America has made possible the most significant middle class in history, an unprecedented opportunity for common families to make their way in the world. Our scientific and technological work has placed us at the forefront of inventions, cures, and discoveries. The American economy has afforded Americans the ability to contribute to charity here and abroad at levels unmatched by any other economy in the world. Although America is a relatively new society, it has led significantly with its artistic and entertainment work: Our writers, from Melville and Twain to Fitzgerald and Hemingway, have set standards for the modern novel; Poe is largely credited with the development of the short story as a genre. Hollywood became synonymous with film, Broadway with theater. Jazz, country, gospel, and rock all evolved here. Through unprecedented philanthropy some of the world's greatest museums and orchestras emerged here in America and have showcased our leading artists: the painters Thomas Eakins, Mary Cassat, and Edward Hopper, for instance; musical performers, such as Marion Anderson, Itzhak Perlman, and Yo-Yo Ma; and, among our leading composers, Samuel Barber, Aaron Copland, and Leonard Bernstein.

Our memory is formed by the *courage* that sustained the founders who risked their fortunes and their lives and who, with their vision and valor, established the most enduring constitutional republic in history. We honor the courage of the men and women who ran the Underground Railroad and the courage of American servicemen who won World War II, nearly 12.5 million of them enlisted by 1945. As a nation we have held first responders in high esteem. In the days around 9/11, for example, the firemen and policemen who served and the many who died at Ground Zero became our national heroes; their heroism is now permanently revered in the 9/11 Memorial and Museum in New York City. As individuals, families, and associations, we are grateful as well for all the legal and political efforts to advance equality and freedom for all Americans across our history.

Americans hold a place in their hearts for courageous trailblazers: Lewis and Clark, the exemplars of "undaunted courage," traversing the American wilderness in 1803-1806;[49] the thousands of teachers, especially women, who braved sparse wages, isolated locations and spartan facilities in order to educate America's growing primary and secondary student population in the 1800s; the homesteading families of the 1850s on; Clara Barton, who pioneered nursing in the most arduous of circumstances during the Civil War; the Wright

---

[49] Stephen Ambrose, *Undaunted Courage: Meriwether Lewis, Thomas Jefferson, and the Opening of the American West* (New York: Simon & Schuster, 1996).

brothers; the wildcat oilmen of early 1900s Texas; and the "right stuff" astronauts of the 1960s, just to name a few.[50]

Americans share all kinds of recognizable loves: They love family and home. Their peace and contentment have mostly to do with providing for their families; their hopes for the future have largely to do with improving life for their children. Americans love the second chances or fresh opportunities afforded tens of millions of immigrants; the dramatic skylines of our big cities; the small towns, majestic mountains, open skies, and national parks of our bucolic landscape; cars and the open road; hard work, competition, and invention; sports, music, and movies; and taking the lead in every kind of important human venture from building the biggest economy in the world to landing the first man on the moon.

Americans love freedom. The history of the country is really the history of our quest for the freedom to establish and develop ourselves as a self-governing people, to advance freedom to all our members, and to be a beacon of freedom to the world. And, while that quest has at times devolved from freedom, the force of the founding principles, the sacrifice made in the Civil War to end slavery and to re-unite American society, the century-long struggle to end segregation, and the victorious defense against fascist, imperialist, and communist assaults on Western civilization all speak of a remarkable quest for freedom and a land worthy of love.

---

[50] Tom Wolfe, *The Right Stuff* (New York: Farrar, Straus and Giroux, 1979).

There is one final love to note, and this one is, in some ways, the most significant: Americans are deeply religious, and at the foundation of their religiosity is a vast and unabashed expression of love for God. We have been deeply religious from our beginnings. A religious imagination has shaped our responses to national crises. Never has there been a country with such a wide variety of religions co-existing. No people gives so generously as Americans do through charity for the sake of their neighbors at home and abroad—this, a direct corollary to their faith.

Work, courage, and love: These are sources of meaning. Our recollection of events that express those sources most significantly are not the only kinds of things we remember. We remember troubling events as well and regret our failures. Nor do all of us recall meaningful events with the same level of importance. What each person praises and what each recoils from will depend, to some significant degree, on his or her personal experience. Nevertheless, the work, courage, and love that mark our society's signature events are what give our collective existence some recognizable meaning. If we are to maintain our existence, we must find meaning not in ignoble acts but in noble ones: fostering justice, not injustice; living in sympathy for others rather than in domination; creating opportunity and unity in place of division.

That we continue to accept and cultivate life based on good memories is true for individuals and for societies. These higher ideals, the nobler achievements, and the genuine sacrifices made for others and for the common good indicate a society's most important historical movement. For example, in World

War II, America went from being a sleeping giant, caught unprepared at Pearl Harbor, to becoming the principal leader and victor against the Axis Powers. Combined with the leading role we assumed during the Cold War, that rise heralded America's arrival as the "leader of the free world." Such purpose, of course, is defined largely by the context. In the case of World War II, the threat of the Axis powers formed one major part of the context; the threat of communism during the Cold War, especially the threat posed by Soviet Russia, formed another. As students today increasingly forget either set of related events, their evaluation of America's historical role and purpose is shifting as well. The division from their past constitutes a loss of understanding and of meaning.

Remembering What We Did Not Live

We have noted one important distinction between individual and public memory: that an individual is more unified as a remembering subject than a society. Another distinction to bear in mind is that a society does not remember in the same way an individual does. Of my life, I can only remember what I lived, extending back across a handful of decades. Through history, we, the living members of a society, remember by and large what we did not live. Among the events we recall as Americans, some extend back in time to the founding, such as the signing of the Declaration of Independence in 1776. Some reach even further back to England, especially to the sources of our legal and political traditions, as in the case of the English Bill of Rights in 1689 and the Magna Carta in 1215. Some events we recollect occurred across the range of our ancestral homelands and have forged our cultural practices. Other events reach us today from across millenia and our civilizational origins. There in antiquity, formative features were born, such as democratic practice and ideals, biblical symbols, and Roman architecture. Each has left a residual imprint on our culture.

Note that all these examples situate history among people. History rests chiefly in a society or civilization, secondarily in smaller groups such as families. It is not entirely accurate, then, to say that ideas have history. Only in a limited way can we say that an area of the earth, as such, has history. True, geologists speak of the antiquity of the earth, and cartographers capture historical changes in political and economic geography. At the same time, the earth is not conscious and, therefore, does not have the capacity to remember. Political maps only emerge in relation to historical cultures. Only people have history.

Nor is it accurate to suggest that history judges or will judge us. Only persons are capable of judgment. History itself has no standing as an agent; only persons do. True, it is likely that future historians will write about our times and evaluate our actions, and some people believe, as a matter of faith, that all humans will in the future stand before an eternal judge. History as such, however, will not judge; it will no more act than any field of study or concept can act.

No academic subject, no form of recollection, and no idea has personality or agency; none can do anything. In any expression of what history is, it has no memory of what has happened. People have history, and only people find meaning through the recollection of their past.

VI. Meaning Forgotten

If the Russian people and the Russian elite remembered - viscerally, emotionally remembered - what Stalin did to the Chechens, they could not have invaded Chechnya in the 1990s, not once and not twice. To do so was the moral equivalent of postwar Germany invading western Poland. Very few Russians saw it that way—which is itself evidence of how little they know about their own history.

—Anne Applebaum

As recollection has the great potential to fill life with meaning, forgetfulness can portend its loss. Think here of a man who suffers from forgetfulness as a function of age or malady; the loss of memory creates a dry gulf in his self-knowledge. That separation extends to our relationship with him as communication becomes increasingly difficult. We say of an individual who loses her temper, *she forgot herself*, of someone who neglects his roots, *he has forgotten where he came from*. Such a loss can be temporary, or it might indicate a decline from which one never recovers.

History and Responsibility

As an individual needs to remember who she is in order to do what she needs to do, a people's unity of purpose requires public memory as well:

When in the course of human events…
Remember the Alamo!
Four score and seven years ago…

These three memorable lines invoke the past for the sake of unified action in the present. Another, the Holocaust motto, *Never Again*, invokes the past in a permanent charge to never forget what conditions fueled the Shoah and what responses offered too little resistance or none at all. The effect of such a charge rests on an understanding of universal human dignity, a shared commitment to build a culture of life and equality, and the willingness to generously and courageously defend each person. By such true remembrance we are free to act with concerted effort in the face of mortal threats. Forgetfulness, by contrast, strains that ability and leaves our existence exposed.

The meaning that develops through memory rests in significant measure on the completeness of historical observation; and action, to be well-founded, must be born from a grasp of historical reality. Primacy has to lie with understanding. A university establishes a course on the history of the Vietnam War in order to shape the understanding of young men and women. Secondarily, but importantly, the university knows that its graduates will impact the order of their society and, having studied the past, will, with the wisdom afforded them by that study, responsibly face comparable events in the future. For similar reasons, the Holocaust Museum was founded: to deepen the public's understanding of past events in hopes that a historically minded public will prevent a recurrence of the Shoah and the conditions that led to it.

Note that either kind of enterprise first shapes our understanding. Then, as a habit of mind, historical understanding forms our memory and provides a reasonable and therefore necessary foundation for how we meet our responsibilities. Recollection is a precondition for acting. Memory without understanding is like opinion without knowledge, unmoored and vulnerable to manipulation or loss. If built on understanding, memory penetrates to true meaning, deepens the sympathy we have for the human condition, and strengthens our willingness to act according to what is truly good. Understood rightly, history is not a source that incites but a source for deliberation. To deliberate is to consider right means toward good ends, which are identifiable in light of what is already experienced and known as truly good. In its relation to history, unified action is not chiefly a break with the past, a break that is either assumed or intended, but chiefly the preservation and improvement of the public order.

Action that stems from observation, understanding, and deliberation should not be confused with action born from the selective reduction of past events, the redefinition of history as a revolutionary force, or the summary judgment of existing order. In its generally accepted meaning, the radical call to "change the world" does not rest on historical understanding and is not born from deliberation concerning right means toward good ends; nor is it built on an acceptance of our historical existence as fundamentally good. Changing the world, radically conceived, opposes cultivation—the preservation and improvement of what McClay calls the "human things" necessary to our existence as a lasting society.

Forgetfulness and Division

We are all witnesses to forgetfulness at work in our contemporary national culture. We are increasingly divided from our past and from one another. Our forgetfulness severs us from our origins at the American Founding and in the foundations of the West; it severs our bonds to one another. Today, the two kinds of harm seem to be occurring at the same time.

For example, on the matter of our historical continuity, one side of our cultural divide looks to the American Founding—the formative events between independence in 1776 and the ratification of the Constitution in 1788—as the enduring source of America's origins. The other dispenses with those events, fixes our beginning at the emergence of American slavery in 1619, then proceeds to reinterpret our existence in terms of slavery and racism and our most formative events and ideals in terms of the first slaves and their descendants.[51]

For another related example, Western culture, once the heart of American education, is increasingly scrubbed from American curricula as if its prevalence in our past and relevance today are no longer worth examining or, worse yet, itself a

---

[51] Nikole Hannah-Jones, lead essay, *The 1619 Project, The New York Times* online, August 2019, https://www.nytimes.com/interactive/2019/08/14/magazine/1619-america-slavery.

form of oppression. Although the West was historically the source of a coherent rationale for studying all historical cultures, the study of the West now gives way to alternative cultural studies—contemporary expressions of sub-group identity. In this approach, the historian's emphasis on what is different about the past—understood contextually—gives way to what is different about each class, gender, and race, abstracted from full historical context and typically focused on the respective group's experience of exploitation. Change that brought us to this day concedes the ground to the active pursuit of change today. Cultural *studies* are largely a substitute for what used to be the study of culture within the *disciplines* of the humanities and as the shared record and practices that society holds sacred.[52] In other words, cultural tribalism displaces a culture we all hold in common.

Among other current events, these two revisions of our historical origins—the one that shifts our beginning from the American Founding to the emergence of American slavery, the other that displaces Western culture with cultural studies—indicate that we are losing a shared understanding of who we are as Americans and Westerners. We are, in other words, increasingly divided from each other. Again, we need to find a common ground.

---

[52] John Heath, "More Quarreling in the Muses' Birdcage," in *Bonfire of the Humanities: Rescuing the Classics in an Impoverished Age*, ed. John Heath, Victor Davis Hanson, and Bruce Thornton (Wilmington: ISI Books, 2001), 55-92.html.

Forgetfulness and Domination

Forgetfulness takes on yet greater gravity when it is wed to more expansive, more coercive attempts to change human nature. For example, in order to keep Russian culture within the constraints of historical materialism, a centerpiece of Soviet ideology, Soviet authorities systematically assaulted sources of meaning for the Russian people: religion, family, and history itself. Civil ceremonies displaced Christian weddings and baptisms, and Russian churches were forced to subject themselves to state control or face violent persecution. Family members were divided from each other as they gave in to the state's pressure to spy on one another. Entire historical archives were removed; topics, such as the Russian famine under Stalin, were forbidden; and Soviet texts and encyclopedias were updated repeatedly according to the latest shifts in the Party ideology.[53] Robert Conquest explains this "falsification" imposed on history as one of two major tactics used to dominate the Russian people. The other was terror:

> Was the terror intrinsic? Was it necessary? Perhaps only by such methods could the regime enforce its irrational policies.
>
> All in all, unprecedented terror must seem necessary to ideologically motivated attempts to transform society massively and speedily, against its natural possibilities. The accompanying falsification took place... in every sphere. Real facts, real statistics, disappeared

[53] Robert Conquest, *Reflections on a Ravaged Century* (New York: Norton, 2000), 101.

> into the realm of fantasy. History, including the history of the Communist Party, or rather especially the history of the Communist Party, was rewritten. Unpersons disappeared from the official record. A new past, as well as a new present, was imposed on the captive minds of the Soviet population, as was, of course, admitted when truth emerged in the late 1980s.[54]

When we forget who and what we are under the imposition of a "new past" and a "new present," we lose our meaning; without meaning, our existence is in peril. This is why history is a necessary, vital part of a liberal education, an education to freedom.

[54] Robert Conquest, *Reflections on a Ravaged Century*, 101.

VII. History As One

Society is a partnership in all science; a partnership in all art; a partnership in every virtue and in all perfection. As the ends of such a partnership cannot be obtained in many generations, it becomes a partnership not only between those who are living, but between those who are dead and those who are to be born.

—Edmund Burke

History is a field of study, a way of interpreting our existence, a framework by which we identify our responsibilities, and a recollective vision where we name those to whom we belong: the dead, the living, and the future generations not yet born. At work in all of those ways of thinking historically, history is also a concept. You may not normally think concepts are the concern of a history teacher, but every teacher uses concepts. We cannot think without them; nor can our students observe, identify and grasp what they are observing in reality without concepts. As it is, it matters greatly how we think about history as we lead our students in discussions. As the section above on Soviet ideology indicates, the wrong conception of history can serve the darkest of purposes. In an attempt to advance our best understanding of history yet further, let us consider more closely history as a concept.

Some concepts speak to particulars. Within the study of history, we speak of particular events or a civilizational component, such as law or region, and each of those is a concept. Some concepts reach for a larger grasp of our existence—for instance, nature and being. Together, these two help us grasp the existence of things: what things are, that they are, and how they all hold together. They are concepts of unity, and they help us reach for the whole of existence or to grasp the whole of things. History is such a concept of unity. It is a concept of a society's whole existence moving in time; and it captures and preserves the when, where, who, and what of a society.[55]

On one level, a society exists in time so that its existence is a matter of continuity between its past, present, and future. A society comes into existence at some point in time, lasts for some duration, and then either ceases to exist or endures. This is the when of human existence.

On another level, a society exists somewhere with a distinctive culture. Each has an identifiable geographic location and a set of distinctive cultural expressions: language, literature, science, law, arts, economy, and religious beliefs and practices. These are the where, who, and what of human existence.

Some history is completed. For example, as a civilization, Ancient Rome no longer exists. As such, it has no continuing

---

[55] Gerhart Niemeyer, "History and Civilization," in *Within and Above Ourselves: Essays of Political Analysis* (Wilmington: ISI Books, 1996), 3.

public memory and, therefore, no shared expectation of its future. We the living remember Rome, sometimes by formal study, as in the accounts of various emperors, sometimes as a matter of continued practice. We formally study and thus remember Rome's expansion and eventual decline. Any history of Rome recounts its engineering feats: the vast network of roads, aqueducts, and famed public spaces, such as the Forum, Colosseum, and Circus Maximus. Sometimes our memory of Rome is a matter of continued practice: for instance, our legal use of the Latin terms, *stare decisis*, *habeas corpus*, and *pro bono*. Yet, despite our current formal study and continued practice, Rome itself no longer is and, thus, no longer remembers.

By contrast, America's history falls into the category of the living and is still developing, as is the West's. Each of these two histories is ongoing because each society continues to exist, and these two histories converge in a shared continuity. In the case of America, we observe when it is, as in our past, present, and future, from the pre-colonial to the present day, and the long-held national conviction that we ought to and can make progress in the future. We observe its location, North America, between the Atlantic and Pacific Oceans, with its variety of terrains and climates. We observe its culture and the most distinctive features that make America what it is: a constitutional democratic republican government, with British political and legal roots; a mixed, free market-regulated economy; a population formed by widely varying groups of immigrants; an admixture of personal independence and public interdependence; a comparatively high level of mobility; and a generally religious populace.[56] The continuity is true even though geographic, demographic, economic, and cultural changes have been extensive.

Because of the constancy of historical change, continuity may be the most difficult feature of history to comprehend. It is not difficult when we consider the facticity of dates; we can rely pretty well on that framework. While the causes of an event are generally points of significant debate, as are consequences, when the event happened is generally not a controversial matter. Around the date of an event, historians carefully fill in other facts so that we can see the event in its most time-bound features. Nor is it difficult to think of history in terms of its strict chronology with each year following another and events occurring in succession.

Finally, continuity is not so difficult to grasp in terms of the continued identity of a society. We speak accurately, for example, of America, France, and Russia as continuous societies in spite of the significant changes that mark their histories: America's comparatively recent emergence as a society; France's five republics since 1789; and Russia's radical shifts between czarist, communist, and authoritarian-presidential regimes.

Here, however, is the difficulty with continuity: The past, the first and primary feature of time, no longer exists; it only was. Nor does the future exist; it only will be. Only the present is,

---

[56] Dalia Fahmy, "Key findings about Americans' belief in God," Pew Research Center, April 25, 2018, https://www.pewresearch.org/fact-tank/2018/04/25/key-findings-about-americans-belief-in-god/.

and even it is fleeting; for, as soon as we say, "now," it passes into the past. Yet, as events such as the Gettysburg Address and the "I Have a Dream" speech demonstrate, past events are clearly more than merely past moments in time. The past, and the still-to-be future that draws on our past, clearly have great force among the living.

VIII. History As Narrative

There is a history in all men's lives.
—Warwick, in William Shakespeare's *Henry V*

In their classic guide, *How to Read a Book*, Mortimer Adler and Charles Van Doren underscore the *story* embedded in history.[57] Narrative history, they argue, is the best way to comprehend history as a genre and as a way of thinking. In fact, the storytelling feature of narrative histories is a chief reason, if not *the* chief reason, they are so appealing to readers. They capture our historical imagination in ways similar to how fiction writers draw us into the imaginative worlds they create.

History-telling

We are by nature storytellers. As the historian John Lukacs reminds us, "[w]e are all by nature historians" as well.[58] Among other things, that means that, in order to understand our humanity, we must grasp our awareness of the past and our articulation of it in story form. When we think historically, we think in terms similar to those we employ in storytelling.

---

[57] Mortimer Adler and Charles Van Doren, *How To Read a Book: The Classic Guide to Intelligent Reading* (New York: Touchstone, 1972), 230.
[58] John Lukacs, *Remembered Past: On History, Historians and Historical Knowledge* (Wilmington: ISI Books, 2005), 4.

Histories have beginnings, middles, and ends. Furthermore, our imaginations are captured by great figures or peoples achieving great deeds or enduring great suffering at times and in places that serve as settings for those great events. In other words, the greatness of past historical events is similar to the dramatic events and characters of a novel or play.

Our history-telling takes different forms: the arrangement of war cemeteries; the grand design of monuments and civic buildings; the displays of artifacts in museums; or the color and pomp of flags, anthems, and public holidays. Some history-telling takes the form of a sacred text in which a people recollects their experience of God. Jews live in remembrance of the events of Exodus, for example, events that forge their remembrance of God's delivering hand and are recounted in the Torah. Christians have at the core of their existence Christ's charge to "do this in memory of me" and to wait for his return with a watchman's eye as it will come like a "thief in the night," both recollections reported in the New Testament.

History-telling touches our imaginative works of literature as well. Homer's epics and Aeschylus' tragedies come to mind as stories whose events were shaped by the Greeks' recollective experiences and stories that shaped Greek historical consciousness. Dante's *Divine Comedy*, Shakespeare's history plays, and novels such as Dickens' *Tale of Two Cities* or Solzhenitsyn's *One Day in the Life of Ivan Denisovich* achieve similar ends. None of these are history as such, but each is informed by history, and each shapes how readers think of life lived in light of the past.

The less formal kinds of history-telling are not negligible in our understanding of what history is as a way of interpreting our existence. They actually have a claim to a kind of primacy over formal history. Historians reconstruct past events, but those events have already been narrated in some form or another.[59] In other words, it is not history as the field of study that comes first; rather, the past and our awareness of it come first. All this speaks to our nature and our condition: We are historical creatures who live under the influence of the past. In this respect, Lucaks' claim that we are all historians is accurate.

Then, there is the formal, written study of the past. Within this last form, narrative history is understood in the narrower sense of the work of historians.

Inside a Narrative

There are three general features of narrative history:

> (1) Like a story, a narrative history has a beginning, a middle, and an end.
> (2) It focuses on extraordinary events.
> (3) The main, though not exclusive, focus of narrative history is politics. The movement of the whole of a society is best captured in political history, the most comprehensive historical branch. By focusing chiefly on politics,

[59] David Walsh, *The Politics of Person as the Politics of Being* (Notre Dame: University of Notre Dame Press, 2016), 188.

narrative history thereby cultivates the student's grasp of history as a concept of unity.

There are four specific or constitutive features of narrative history as well. Narrative historians build their works with these ingredients:[60]

(1) Data—comparative levels of peacetime troops in France, Germany, and Russia prior to World War I, for instance,[61] or comparative GDPs among all the Allies and Axis Powers during World War II.[62]
(2) Images—portraits or photos of important individuals or maps of territorial expansion and military invasion.[63]
(3) Structural analyses—an explanation, for example, of the Constitution or the Presidency as a key structure in American political history.[64]
(4) Individual and group narratives—the diaries kept by colonial Americans,[65] or letters and public resolutions written by American blacks in response to the Civil War's outbreak.[66]

---

[60] Gordon Wood, introductory remarks, "2010 Ruth Ratner Miller Award Lecture with Bernard Bailyn," October 23, 2010, Youtube video, 47:13, "Concord Free Public Library," https://www.youtube.com/watch?v=KvqeBomoZv0.

[61] Eugene Davidson, *The Making of Adolf Hitler: The Birth of and Rise of Nazism* (Columbia: University of Missouri Press, 1977), 52.

[62] Victor Davis Hanson, *The Second World Wars: How the First Global Conflict Was Fought and Won* (New York: Basic Books, 2017), 455.

[63] Donald Kagan, Steven Ozment, and Frank M. Turner, *The Western Heritage Since 1300* (Upper Saddle River: Pearson, 2007), 588, 831, 851, 946 and 1019.

[64] Forrest McDonald, *A Constitutional History of the United States* (Malabar: Robert F. Krieger, 1986); *The American Presidency: An Intellectual History* (Lawrence: University Press of Kansas, 1994).

[65] Morgan, *The Puritan Family*, 5.

[66] James McPherson, *The Negro's Civil War: How American Blacks Felt and Acted During the War for the Union* (New York: Pantheon, 1965), 19-35.

Those seven key features—three general and four constitutive, help us grasp a work of narrative history and focus our minds inside the story. On them, the historian develops the broader narrative and makes an interpretative case for what has happened in the past. Each one allows us to look through the historian's scope to see the movement of human existence in context: when events happened in the past, what type of events they were, and what change the events caused, including the past's residues that are evident around us.

The Drama of History

One of our most popular narrative historians, David McCullough, captures here why narrative history has such exceptional storytelling power—its capacity to grasp the whole of our condition, not just the whole of the time and places of our existence:

> History is about high achievement, glorious works of art, music, architecture, literature, philosophy, science and medicine—not just politics and the military—as the best of politicians and generals have readily attested. History is about leadership, and the power of ideas. History is about change, because the world has never not been changing, indeed because life itself is change. History is the course of human events. And it must therefore be, if truthful, about failure, injustice, struggle, suffering, disappointment, and the humdrum. History demonstrates often in

> brutal fashion the evils of enforced ignorance and demagoguery. History is a source of strength, a constant reminder of the courage of others in times more trying and painful than our own.[67]

Life is a drama, in other words, and history is the action and dialogue of the human story played out in time. The chief stage of action is political because of its exceptional level of comprehensiveness, but as McCullough points out, the full story of our existence encompasses each realm of human experience. How humans respond in historical circumstances is no less dramatic than the fictional stories that claim our imaginations. Indeed, one important reason narrative history works so well and is the benchmark among historical genres is because of its ability to capture the dramatic changes that mark our society moving in time. Narrative history tells the story of the human condition as something not static or narrow but as changing, broad, soaring, wide, and measurably varying—at times glorious and at others the expression of our greatest limitations and darkest failures. It reveals how humans live in between defining poles: The movements of our society shift sometimes toward order, sometimes toward disorder. They are movements back and forth between justice and injustice, war and peace, decline and prosperity. These events are the objects of our observation, the sources of the most meaningful recollection, and the material out of which the most informative stories are constructed.

---

[67] David McCullough, "Appreciation: The Citizen Chronicler," Jefferson Lecture 2003, National Endowment for the Humanities, https://www.neh.gov/about/awards/jefferson-lecture/david-mccullough-biography.

Narrative history captures that sweep of dramatic movement for the history student. It affirms our existence, even in light of our troubling past events. For, without existence first, there is no improvement, no reconciliation at the end of the war, no future where character reigns over prejudice. Finally, because the movement toward order, toward charity and equality, is a matter of great difficulty, history is a source of strength as we recall the heroism of those who gave us both our existence and another day to improve the place we inherited.

IX. The Fragmentary Past

[S]ome historians today are more apt to stress the failures of the [American] Revolution. As one young historian recently put it, the Revolution "failed to free the slaves, failed to offer full political equality to women, failed to grant citizenship to Indians, [and] failed to create an economic world in which all could compete on equal terms." Such anachronistic statements suggest a threshold of success that no eighteenth century revolution could possibly have attained, and perhaps tell us more about the political attitudes of the historians who make such statements than they do about the American Revolution.

—Gordon S. Wood

History in general and narrative history specifically, are increasingly under siege. This assault is a reflection of the times, a window into our increasingly divided culture, and a symptom of the declining study of the humanities. As teachers, we need to grasp the situation in order to navigate the difficult terrain our students and we are facing. One of our best practitioners of narrative history, Brown University's Gordon Wood, has this to say about the problematic development as it appears among academic historians:

> [I]nstead of writing full-scale narrative histories, the new generation of historians has devoted itself to isolating and recovering stories of the dispossessed: the women kept in dependence; the American Indians

> shorn of their lands; the black slaves brought in chains from Africa. Consequently, much of their history is fragmentary and essentially anachronistic—condemning the past for not being more like the present. It has no real interest in the pastness of the past.[68]

Note the two major flaws that Wood identifies in fragmentary history:

> (1) It "isolates" events by taking them out of context.
> (2) It "[condemns] the past for not being more like the present."

Of course, Wood is in no way hinting that somehow dispossession, domination and slavery are not real, nor am I. It is a real evil to categorize and reduce people to less than fully human, then enslave, displace, or suppress them. Still, examined in their full historical contexts, past events as objects of study are not occasions for anachronistic moral denunciations, nor primarily a cause for action; rather, within the discipline of history, they are primarily occasions for observation and for developing our understanding.

That is true even in the case of American slavery. Note, for example, the liberal approach taken by Yale's Edmund S. Morgan in his study of two great opposing features of America's founding: American slavery and American freedom, which developed at the same time and in no small measure in

---

[68] Gordon S. Wood, "History in Context," *Washington Examiner*, February 23, 2015, www.washingtonexaminer.com/weekly-standard/history-in-context.

interdependence.[69] This is especially evident in Virginia, where leading founders were also slaveholders. However, in spite of Virginia's slave culture, and in spite of the compromise struck between the northern founders and their fellow founders in the south, Morgan does not dismiss the founding as morally vacuous nor the Virginia founders as depraved.[70] He takes the founders at their word concerning freedom, even the voices of freedom in Virginia, where figures no less than Washington, Jefferson, Madison, Monroe, and Mason owned slaves. He lets neither reality obscure or negate the other. As painful as it is to recognize the relationship between the two features, Morgan leaves the relationship between them as a paradox. In his liberal approach to American history, he keeps his eye focused on the formative roles slavery *and* freedom have had in the founding, the devolution to civil war, the century-long struggle for integration, and the nation's ongoing quest for equality of freedom.

Opposed to the liberal approach that studies the past because it is different, the "fragmentary" approach to history studies the past because it is morally objectionable. Instead of reading an event in its context, fragmentary history either isolates the moral offense from other factors, thereby diminishing the fuller context, or permits the offense to obscure the other factors. In either kind of reduction, the net result is not an inquiry into historical reality, at least not an inquiry into the full reality. Fragmentary history may compellingly focus on what Bailyn calls the "troubling" events we remember, but its

[69] Edmund S. Morgan, *American Slavery, American Freedom* (New York: Norton, 1975).
[70] Morgan, American Slavery, *American Freedom*, 375-376.

focus is executed in a manner that marginalizes other events we would "embrace." As a consequence, the broader human condition is given deficient consideration, and our sympathy for that condition is diminished.

Slavery Out of Context

A form of the fragmentary approach has caught a strong wind in popular American history. We see fragmentation throughout the *1619 Project*, cited earlier in this book in the chapter on forgetfulness. While self-identified as journalism, the *Project* has been marketed to schools for use in the teaching of history. In the authors' retelling of the past, 1619 displaces 1776 and the American Founding as the time America was born on the grounds that it is the year the first African slaves arrived on American soil. Then, in a sweeping reworking of events, *all* subsequent American history is reinterpreted from the vantage point of this initial, defining exploitation:

> [T]he consequences of slavery and the contributions of black Americans [are placed] at the very center of the story we tell ourselves about who we are as a country.[71]

Because of slavery, the *Project* summarily declares, the ideals of the founding are "false" and collectively a "lie."

[71] Jake Silverstein, "Why We Published the 1619 Project," *1619 Project, The New York Times* online, December 20, 2019, https://www.nytimes.com/interactive/2019/12/20/magazine/1619-intro.html.

Consequently, traditional sources of authority, especially the Declaration of Independence and the Constitution, are displaced. At the same time, "[b]lack Americans have," despite the founding, "fought to make [those ideals] true."[72] In other words, the ideals are removed from their context and their veracity made dependent on an alternative set of events.

We see here the fragmentary approach at work. First, the moral offense is clearly identified, namely slavery. Then, it displaces other events that would otherwise be observed within the scope of history and provide meaning and purpose as a matter of public memory. Finally, the past is retold as an extension of the original moral failure.

Among the *Project*'s other fragmentary symptoms, the following were identified by a group of prominent American historians, including Gordon Wood, in a public letter they wrote to the *New York Times* where the *Project* is housed:

> On the American Revolution, pivotal to any account of our history, the project asserts the founders declared independence of Britain "in order to ensure that slavery would continue."
>
> [T]hat "for the most part," black Americans have fought their freedom struggles "alone."

---

[72] Nikole Hannah-Jones, lead essay, *1619 Project*, *The New York Times* online, August 14, 2019, https://www.nytimes.com/interactive/2019/08/14/magazine/black-history-american-democracy.html.

> The project criticizes Lincoln's views on racial equality but ignores his conviction that the Declaration of Independence proclaimed universal equality, for blacks as well as whites, a view he upheld repeatedly against white supremecists who opposed him.
>
> The project also ignores Lincoln's agreement with Frederick Douglass that the Constitution is a "GLORIOUS LIBERTY DOCUMENT." Instead, the project asserts that the United States was founded on racial slavery, an argument rejected by the majority of abolitionists [but] accepted by champions of slavery like John C. Calhoun.[73]

In other words, the *Project* makes exaggerated claims, leaves out important relevant facts and details, and rests on a moralistic dismissal of the founding. The net effect is to displace the study of slavery from its proper historical context. The displacement worsens when we consider other omissions; or, to put this constructively, a broader, comparative history of slavery would go a long way to restore slavery to its proper context.

---

[73] Victoria Bynum, James M. McPherson, James Oakes, Sean Wilentz, Gordon S. Wood, "RE: The 1619 Project," *The New York Times Magazine*, December 29, 2019, quoted in Jake Silverstein, "Letter to the Editor: We Respond to the Historians Who Critiqued The 1619 Project," *The New York Times* online, last updated January 4, 2020, https://www.nytimes.com/2019/12/20/magazine/we-respond-to-the-historians-who-critiqued-the-1619-project.html. Subsequent to the publication of the historians' letter, the *Project* pared back its claim that the founders intended independence as a means to preserve slavery.

For one thing, the institution of slavery existed and stood generally uncriticized for thousands of years prior to the American Revolution.[74] Slavery was well-established as part of African social structures before the American slave trade developed.[75] A full millennium prior to 1619, black Africans were enslaved by Arabs to their north.[76] The British began trading in African slaves in the 1500s.[77] On the other side of American slavery, and more than a century and a half after its abolition here, slavery continues today in much of the non-Western world; and American legal practices are being utilized at the frontline of the fight against the modern day slave trade.[78]

Secondly, the American Revolution set in motion an abolition movement that was unprecedented in world history. Because of that movement, for the first time southern slaveholders felt pressured to defend the institution of slavery. On the one hand, some steeled their defense of slavery; among them, their defensiveness hardened in light of the revolts in Haiti and Virginia, the former successful, the latter a noble

---

[74] Stewart Gordon, *Shackles of Iron: Slavery Beyond the Atlantic* (Indianapolis: Hacket, 2016), xiii-xxiv; James Walvin, A Short History of Slavery (London: Penguin Books, 2007), 7-34.
[75] John Thornton, *Africa and Africans in the Making of the Atlantic World*, 1400-1800 (New York: Cambridge University Press, 2011),72-97.
[76] Bernard Lewis, *Race and Slavery in the Middle East: An Historical Enquiry* (New York: Oxford Press, 1990), 16-20, 28-36.
[77] F.A. Halliday, *A Concise History of England: From Stonehenge to the Atomic Age* (London: Thames and Hudson, 1989), 99.
[78] On the contemporary slave trade, see https://www.globalslaveryindex.org/2018/findings/highlights/. On American juridical work in the fight against modern slavery, see https://www.ijm.org/our-work. On the slave uprisings in Haiti and Virginia, see Walvin, *A Short History of Slavery* (London: Penguin Books, 2007), 158-159, and David Brion Davis, *Inhuman Bondage: The Rise and Falls of Slavery in the New World* (New York, Oxford University Press, 2006), 207-211.

failure. On the other hand, under the same abolitionist pressure, some southern slaveholders issued manumissions.[79]

Thirdly, America and Britain outlawed the slave trade in the same year, 1807, decades after America declared independence; the British only effectively ended slavery in the empire in 1833, almost a half century after the American Revolution.[80] Both events remind us how entirely implausible it is that the Americans declared their independence in 1776 in order to preserve slavery.

Finally, there is the Civil War. While abolition was not initially a major rationale for the war, it became one for Lincoln and the North. No other country in the history of the world has fought a civil war and expended so many lives over slavery. In other words, while black Africans paid the first terrible price for American slavery, America as a whole paid the second.

None of the historical factors included here are meant to diminish either the injustice of American slavery or the extent of suffering endured by American slaves. Their inclusion is intended to suggest a better alternative to the fragmentary approach of the *1619 Project*—better, because it would be significantly truer to the past and, therefore, to what followed. If we want history students to understand American slavery,

---

[79] Tom Mackaman, "An Interview with Historian Gordon Wood on the New York Times' 1619 Project," World Socialist Web Site, International Committee of the Fourth International, November 28, 2019, https://www.wsws.org/en/articles/2019/11/28/wood-n28.html. On the leading role played by Americans in the abolition movement here and in Britain, see Walvin, A Short History of Slavery, 147-152.

[80] Halliday, *A Concise History of England*, 174.

especially at its most critical junctures—1619, the founding, the Civil War, and abolition—then we need to restore the relevant events to the context in which they and their legacy are all sufficiently observable.

America Out of Context

On an even larger scale, fragmentation is the heart of the most popular work on American history, Howard Zinn's *The People's History of the United States.*[81] His story interprets the past from the vantage point of all groups exploited as classes, races, and genders. In order to execute his interpretation, Zinn displaces the unity of American society:

> My viewpoint, in telling the history of the United States, is different: that we must not accept the memory of states as our own. Nations are not communities and never have been. The history of any country . . . conceals fierce conflicts of interest (sometimes exploding, most often repressed) between conquerors and conquered, masters and slaves, capitalists and workers, dominators and dominated in race and sex. And in such a world of conflict, a world of victims and executioners, it is the job of thinking people . . . not to be on the side of the executioners.[82]

---

[81] Howard Zinn, *A People's History of the United States* (New York: Harper Collins, 2003).
[82] Zinn, *A People's History*, 10.

In other words, Zinn's major premise is that we are inherently divided from one another. He asks his readers to reimagine America: Stop thinking of it as a whole society or as a continuous society; think of America in terms of subgroups, as if each of us is defined by our class, race, and gender and as though we are in a struggle against one another. In that imaginative account, each event is reduced to an exploitative event and retold within the chronicled collection of exploitations. For Zinn, it is not important that America as a society moves in time; it is important that history is moving.[83] Within that framework, each of us takes a place on either the right or wrong side of history's "rush" forward.[84] Definitively, we are either "victims" or "executioners," the exploited or the exploiters.

For Zinn, no authoritative source in American history provides meaning or purpose in a way that surmounts the fundamental disunity of our existence; no past event, person, or institution "can represent the nation as a whole."[85] Those who maintain that there is a whole America and that there are sources that can represent us as a society are attempting to see events from what Zinn considers to be a foundational falsehood:

> The pretense is that there really is such a thing as 'the United States'. . . [that is] fundamentally a community of people with common interests. It is as if there really is a 'national interest' represented in the

[83] Zinn, *A People's History*, 9.
[84] Zinn, *A People's History*, 687.
[85] Zinn, *A People's History*, 9.

> Constitution, in territorial expansion, in the laws passed by Congress, the decisions of the courts, the development of capitalism, the culture of education and the mass media.[86]

In the place of any expression of American unity, there is, for Zinn, only American division, struggle, and exploitation. And because the exploited have the only possible moral ground in an existence so narrowly defined, Zinn writes *all* of American history from their perspective, starting with the indigenous peoples encountered by the first Europeans who arrived in the New World. As Columbus' victims and, therefore, the first in the "people's" story, the Arawaks are America's exploited, writ small.[87] Any member of any class, race, or gender who shares a place alongside them as victim or ally is on the right side of history, the people; everyone else is written off as either an oppressor or as complicit in systemic oppression.

Given his starting point—our intractable disunity—Zinn's history is, oddly, not really a history of America as such. America is, more accurately, the collection of traditions, institutions, prejudices, practices, and powerful and wealthy individuals under whose oppression the exploited live. The people are set in opposition to that collection of forces; America as it stands is a field of struggle where the people are on the exploited end of society. At the same time, the people are not entirely aware of their status. And that brings us to

---

[86] Zinn, *A People's History*, 9.
[87] Zinn, *A People's History*, 10.

the role of the *People's History*. Zinn's express purpose is to change America. We can understand the change as unfolding in three stages:

(1) "[A]waken a greater consciousness of class conflict, racial injustice, sexual inequality, and national arrogance."[88]
(2) Displace a shared sense of meaning and purpose found in traditional American sources.[89]
(3) Imagine a "new kind of revolution" toward a new kind of society.[90]

Change here is not the cultivation of what exists already, nor is it an event by which our collective existence survives. There is no impulse in Zinn to preserve or improve American society. Change for him means revolution, and revolution means that America as it is now must be replaced with another society yet to emerge. So much does he see our past as tied to exploitative events that nothing in American history as such warrants Zinn's reverence. Only the endgame, revolution, and the radically new American society it is destined to bring about deserve commitment.

Change as Given Replaced by Change as Purpose

In the liberal approach to history, change is a given, not a goal; it is another way to name the movement or the events

[88] Zinn, *A People's History*, 686 for the quotation. At the same time, Zinn's entire text is a catalogue of events intended to raise consciousness.
[89] Zinn, *A People's History*, 8-10.
[90] Zinn, *A People's History*, 621-641. The chapter title is "The Coming Revolt of the Guards."

of which history consists. If we understand history as a disciplined reconstruction of the past, change is not a cause for action; change is an object of study. Is it more than that? Yes, it is. After all, the memory of change in past events works on us in ways that penetrate to the meaning of our existence as a society. Among other things, whenever we consider what it is to live meaningfully, the consideration of which rests significantly in memory, our responsibility becomes clear. Genuine responsibility, however, rests on a recognition and acceptance of our existence, the goodness of what we share, our bond to one another as persons, and the continuation of who we are as a society. In other words, it rests on the human condition that is ours together, not the alternative condition identified for us as subcultural groups, which, in the fragmentary approach, are typically defined as opposed to each other, even implacably so.

Narrative history is certainly not uncritical of the past. One cannot read Bailyn and Morgan on American slavery, for example, or McClay on the displacement of Native Americans and maintain that any of them embraces the respective egregious injustices. Nor can one read the scholarly criticisms of the *1619 Project* and construe the critics as unsympathetic to the real suffering of black Americans.[91] At the same time, narrative history retains a proper distance from the past and a reverence for its difference, for how it brings us to the world

---

[91] Bynum, McPherson, Oakes, Wilentz, Wood, "RE: The 1619 Project," quoted in Silverstein, "Letter to the Editor: We Respond to the Historians Who Critiqued The 1619 Project"; "Twelve Scholars Critique the 1619 Project and the New York Times Magazine Editor Responds," History News Network, George Washington University, January 26, 2020, https://historynewsnetwork.org/article/174140.

we inhabit now, and for its presence among us. That is the liberal disposition without which history as a field of study becomes something other than a source of knowledge and understanding.

Fragmentary history, by contrast, is reductively critical and, by virtue of its moralism, overly subjective. The fragmentary approach to history reflects the broader displacement of Western culture in favor of cultural studies, a shift that is at once narrow and divisive. It is narrow in that America and the West are not examined in their fullness but primarily, sometimes exclusively, for their moral failures. It is narrow in that people are not observed in the context of their shared culture where culture is understood as a given and necessary good—an arrangement that makes existence possible; rather, they are explored in the narrower context of exploitative events. It is divisive in that persons are reduced to the status of standard-bearers for the right or wrong side of history where history is narrowly defined as the record of subcultural struggles between classes, races, and genders.

Finally, fragmentary history substitutes change as a cause to act—as in revolt—for change as a given reality to be studied in its full context. Among other things, this makes America unobservable as a whole society moving in time. Rather, the struggle for racial, class, and gender ascendancy becomes the narrower, more selective story. In this vein, if there is any change that is true in history, it lies chiefly in the action of the exploited acting against the exploiters. Fragmentary history holds that the complete field of changes (events) constituting

America's past holds out no normative purpose, no meaningful end—this, in spite of the fact that our past includes freedom *and* slavery, slavery *and* emancipation, segregation *and* integration. The fragmentary approach also neglects historical changes that made America the widest sought-after land of opportunity in all of history and a beacon of hope for people of all backgrounds, a reality that continues today and shows no signs of waning.

Denying the Ground on Which We Stand

Exploitation of any kind, especially slavery, is not a human good; on its own, therefore, it cannot provide moral direction. A moral response would have to rest on some good—freedom, justice, dignity, love, or solidarity. By any of those standards, we can call exploitation an evil and find our way to improve the order of society. However, on its own, exploitation can only be a cause of division, suffering, alienation, cynicism, and despair; it cannot be a source of meaning or purpose, for on its own, exploitation offers no good. What could offer meaning or purpose within the scope of fragmentary history? It cannot be society for, at least in the case of America, society is not an existing good but, rather, a field of exploitation. For the *1619 Project*, whatever principles and institutions of freedom American society might encompass are of little or no significance because they were conceived as "false." For the *People's History*, if America is somehow moving toward the one possible good, the end of exploitation, it is not because of society. It is because of history itself, construed as a force or agent, and because of those who are on the right side of history, construed as helping to bring about the change needed to achieve history's purpose.

In the meantime, the fragmentary vision sees no significant meaning to our existence as a whole society with our collective past. There is nothing sacred to revere about America, such as the fallen who died for the country and were remembered by Lincoln at Gettysburg. Nor do promise and hope exist as in King's "I Have a Dream" speech, built as it is on the founding's core principles. In other words, there is nothing substantially good about America as such—nothing inherently good to move us forward in continuity with our past. Built as it is on a body of "false" ideals, America's past is reduced; at most, it is only remembered to be judged and rejected—severed from us as a source of existence, meaning, and purpose. In spite of what Lincoln and King proclaim, those who dedicate their lives to American freedom and equality, as conceived at the founding, misplace their dedication.

The fragmentary form of history neither observes the past in full nor allows the past to work on us in any sustaining way since the abiding commitment opposes the inheritance and cultivation of the historical existence we have received. At most, fragmentary history inspires change; more accurately, it incites radical change. By design, fragmentation upends the foundations, the continuity, and the goodness of our historical existence. By reducing history to less than what it is, fragmentary history ends up being untrue to who we are.

By contrast, a liberal approach to history allows for all questions and expects the fullest range and content in its answers. In no way does it ignore oppression, but neither does it divorce events of oppression from the broader history of America, the West, or any society. History is a wide field, not narrow. Maintaining its liberally wide scope, our net estimation of things will not likely rise to the thrill of activism. Still, the more modest approach is exactly what is warranted. Our job as history teachers is to lead our students according to the truest account of the past, not according to an activist agenda that willfully narrows the account. History as a field of study offers no Jacobin vision; we should not either.

X. The Purposeful Past

I base my sense of the certain overthrow of slavery, in part, upon the nature of the American Government, the Constitution, the tendencies of the age, and the character of the American people... I know of no soil better adapted to the growth of reform than American soil. I know of no country where the conditions for affecting great changes in the settled order of things, for the development of right ideas of liberty and humanity, are more favorable than here in these United States.

—Frederick Douglass, responding to the Dred Scott case

It should be clear by now that one particularly hard-hit target of the fragmentary approach to American history is our founding. For one thing, fragmentary historians have overtly or implicitly interpreted the founding as a lie. For another, the fragmentary approach rejects narrative history as inherently teleological. Teleological is not a term likely to emerge in anyone's high-school history course. Normally, the language of teleology is reserved for the ethical arena, especially classical ethics, where human action is directed toward an end, *telos*, and the end is a purpose or the good of action. Those goods can be arranged in a hierarchy of higher and lower goods. That things are directed to ends as hierarchized goods is the language of teleology. What, then, is its role in narrative history?

The Teleology of History

At a foundational level, historical teleology rests on chronology and the continuity of time. Within narrative history, any part of a society's history is read in light of the whole of its history: from its beginning to the present and, either overtly or indirectly, with some consideration for how society has moved ahead. Bailyn calls these the differences that "changed and evolved to create the world we know." That is the way a historical narrative works, progressing as it does along a timeline that begins, proceeds, and arrives at the latest point in time relative to the story. The point here may seem obvious, but it is important to underscore the when, where, who, and what of history. The movement of a society does not happen in abstraction; it happens in the concrete events of the society's existence in time.

In the more important sense, teleology in narrative history reflects the meaning that we recognize in ethics, the meaning that we identify with purpose where purpose gives us a standard by which to measure existence in terms of goodness. In other words, historical teleology means that there is some good inherent in the past that can be maintained, developed further, and fulfilled in later events. That a society moves in time as a whole and in continuity between the past, the present, and the future are necessary preconditions for the fulfillment of purpose. Still, that higher meaning, society's purpose, is the defining end of that historical movement.

Here is an example: In his 1995 essay, "Last Best Hope for What?" that serves as the introduction to a collection of essays on Lincoln's vision of America and its lasting impact, Princeton's James McPherson—the nation's leading historian of the Civil War era—offers an analysis of Lincoln's famous letter to Congress in 1862. It was in that letter that Lincoln called America "the last best hope on earth." McPherson reads the president's line as a fresh expression of an established American conviction born at the founding, a conviction that asserts that ours is a distinctive political experiment, a drama in which government of the people, by the people, and for the people is both a quest and an idea still being tested.

Here we see the two features of teleology at work. The starting point, the founding, is the beginning of a chronological and purposeful movement. In other words, Lincoln was pointing to the more than eight decades of America's history and to the meaning of it. He was interpreting the Civil War as the critical moment in that decades-old, purposeful movement of the country. He thought that America was, in 1863, on the cusp of fulfilling its purpose in some significant measure. The Confederacy had to be defeated in order that the movement be completed. The urgency of that matter required the funds Lincoln requests of Congress in his letter; and the urgency required the moral purpose he articulates.

What, however, does the phrase, "the last best hope," mean? The phrase is implicitly comparative, as in a last attempt among others. What hope did America offer where others did not? The founders clearly perceived the American republic as a new kind of polity. They thought America was distinctive in that it was free from the monarchical, aristocratic, geographic, and economic constraints of Europe's regimes. Lincoln received that insight and viewed the world around him through a similar lens. Compared with the instability of mid-eighteenth-century European and South American politics, America, Lincoln observed, looked like it had the best chance to prove the promise of popular self-government.[92]

Finally, McPherson examines Lincoln's letter to Congress along with its historical background and brings it forward in an estimation of how the American experiment is faring in our own times. In other words, rather than imposing contemporary moral thinking on Lincoln, he allows Lincoln to work on us today. The direction of his analysis is both chronological and purposeful:

> [Lincoln] led the country through the worst of times to a triumph that left America stronger, more free, and more democratic. And that offers a lesson not only for Americans [today] but for 'the whole family of man.'[93]

Having let the founding anchor his history of Lincoln, McPherson then lets the founding and Lincoln's achievements together serve as a measure of present day America. That is a purposeful reading of America where purpose is identified early on in the founding, developed over the course of the country's history, and brought forward to measure its

[92] James M. McPherson, "Last Best Hope for What?," introduction to *"We Cannot Escape History": Lincoln and the Last Best Hope of Earth*, ed. James M. McPherson (Urbana: Illinois University, 1994), 4-7.
[93] McPherson, "Last Best Hope for What?," 12.

present. Purpose, in other words, pertains to the story of the whole of American society's movement in time. Finally, that the purpose extends a lesson to contemporary readers suggests that the purpose can and should guide us in the years ahead. In other words, such a history draws on the past to offer understanding to those in the present. It is not offered as a blueprint, a cause for activism, or a source of empirical prediction. Rather, this kind of history provides a clarity about our purpose as a society: how it developed from its foundings and, as a matter of practical wisdom, how it can sustain and direct our continued existence. Note here how McPherson is operating with history as a concept of unity.

The Integrity of History

This all may sound controversial. If you have heard that history is merely a matter of facticity or that American history is primarily the occasion to disparage America, you probably will not be surprised to learn that critics of narrative history consider a purposeful or teleological reading as biased. The assumption that there is a purpose to our existence is considered "triumphalist."[94] In other words, the idea that America could have a fulfillment of its promise reflects a prejudice that there is something good about its founding and something lasting in that goodness that either has endured at the heart of America or should have.

---

[94] Wood, "History in Context."

The criticism is moralistic. Because of the evident exploitation at the time of the founding, the criticism goes, there is little or no perceptible good in the founding, or at least none that is defensible in light of what was wrong. The critique expands to cover the entirety of American history so that the central events to recall from our past are the singular moments of exploitation. Those events, since they are divorced from the founding and from any good that is developed from the founding, give the critical historian the alleged evidence for reading American history as the history of exploitation. In other words, the fragmentary approach to history not only reads past events as extracted from their context, it diminishes our public memory by draining it of the meaning and purpose it bears from the founding forward.

If, on the other hand, we follow Bailyn, Wood, Morgan, and McPherson's form of historical thinking, we look back to reconstruct past events in their context, not as isolated events. We trace the changes that led to our world, and we recognize the residues of the past in the present, not as a triumphalism, which would be another kind of moralism, but as the humane occasion to allow the past to work on us through memory, both as something we receive and embrace and as something that is, at times, troubling. In other words, we preserve the integrity of history as a field of study in which the entire story is told, not a fragmentary one intended for ulterior motives.

That preservation of integrity is what the narrative historians do; it is also what the historical figures Lincoln and King do, not as scholars but as public statesmen articulating who we are and what we ought to be according to our founding. All of them exhibit a liberal attitude toward history. Each seeks the truth of history in the past; in that truth, each one provides a foundation for moving forward. Every one of them recognizes the founding as an integral part of our historical existence, not as an opposing one. Theirs is a liberal approach to history, for it is liberal to ask questions and seek answers concerning the common good in terms of the founding, the dignity of each person, and universal equality and freedom. By contrast, it is illiberal to detach ourselves from our beginning as a source of meaning and order.

Fragmentary Teleology

We should note one final feature of the rejection of narrative history as teleological. The fragmentary historian has a teleology as well: The end of history toward which we are supposedly moving is the end of exploitation, the one or ultimate true good envisioned in the fragmentary view.

However, while each of the two views—narrative and fragmentary—is teleological, we should not confuse the one's concept of teleology with the other's. In narrative history, moral reality is a given in both the past and the present. There is good, and the act of telling our history in narrative form is one way we express the basic goodness of our existence. Humans fail, of course, but we also do good things according to the goodness of pre-existing reality. We improve as individuals, and we improve society; and either movement makes sense in light of something already good that is being made better. Further still, the language of *good*, *improve*, and *better* all indicate a moral reality that forms a vital part of the context in which to understand the past and present. Human purpose is born of the intrinsic goodness of existence and of our inherent ability as humans to know what is good, to distinguish it from what is evil, and to live in recognition of both. The intrinsic goodness of existence means, among other things, that our responsibility for one another precedes any evil. In other words, goodness was and is the permanent standard by which to measure all forms of human cruelty, domination, and injustice.

In fragmentary history, the emphases are reversed, the scales tipped: The prevailing feature of the past is human failure; the lone, true good in history lies in the future when the end of exploitation will presumably occur. That teleological view generally vacates the present and the past of their goodness precisely because the founding ideals that would give us purpose are construed as "false." That emptied reality is not reality. Nor as history does it rise to adequately account for our past.

XI. A Past With No Origins

Hear the sum of the whole matter in the compass of one brief word—every art possessed by man comes from Prometheus.
—Prometheus, in Aeschylus' *Prometheus Bound*

There is yet another related layer to the rejection of narrative history. Critics, operating from the fragmentary perspective explored in Chapter IX, typically think that history is nothing more than what humans have done on their own. As a result, they reject narrative history's openness to the full range of sources that run through a society moving in time, including experiences where we discover who we are from beyond ourselves.

Self-creation at the Expense of Others

On the surface, their claim might sound like a reasonable estimation of the past. We are talking about human history; and, further still, only humans have history. Then again, one cannot help but note an exaggeration to the claim. Here is Karl Marx on the matter:

> [S]ince for the socialist man the *entire so-called history of the world* is nothing but the begetting of man through human labour, nothing but the coming-to-be of nature for man, he has the visible, irrefutable

> proof of his *birth* through himself, of his *process* of *coming-to-be*.[95]

In fact, the historical evidence overwhelmingly proves the opposite of Marx's oft-repeated "nothing but" refrain. To start with, no civilization in history has been founded on atheism; every civilization has religious foundations. Morality, law, custom, tradition, art, literature, philosophy, and science have all been rooted in religion in some significant respect. One need not be a believer to recognize religion's civilizational role as a historical fact. Nor need one be a philosopher to recognize the prevalence of events having to do with transcendence—experiences of the true, the good, and the beautiful. Transcendent experiences can be religious or otherwise. In either case, each such experience indicates reality that precedes us and is beyond our making. It seems clear, then, that to narrow human existence to matters of self-creation is at odds with the historical evidence.

What about on the other end of history? If Marx wrongly understood the foundations of society, is it possible his followers brought about the end of oppression? Even a cursory glance at the rise of communist regimes demonstrates that oppression, far from ending, accelerated and increased under the influence of Marx's vision of history. Under Soviet rule alone, more than 20 million Russian subjects, the largest group of which was Ukranian, died from unnatural causes.[96]

---

[95] Karl Marx, *Economic and Philosophic Manuscripts of 1844* (Moscow: Foreign Languages Publishing House, 1956), 112.

[96] Robert Conquest, *The Great Terror: A Reassessment* (New York: Macmillan, 1968), 533.

In Maoist China, approximately 38 million of his country-men fell to his regime's oppression during the Great Leap Forward (1958-1961).[97]

No concept of history has ever resulted in comparable levels of genocide. Nor, when we consider the peasantry targeted by Stalin and Mao, has any concept of history wreaked such carnage among the poor. For at least those reasons, let us examine more closely how Marx's thought regarding history leaves us severed from our origins.

The Self-Creator's Prohibition of Questions

Note Marx's premise: "socialist man." In other words, he frames history and anthropology in socialist terms and limits their scope to those terms exclusively. Elsewhere, Marx reduces all history to class struggle.[98] Today, his intellectual descendants have expanded this notion of history to embrace race, gender, and class struggle; to put it another way, history is the history of exploitation in all its forms. Even in this more inclusive conception, considerations of origins that transcend human self-creation are excluded.

As any student of Marxian thought knows, Marx certainly had his eye on historical movement, specifically what he considered the progressive developments surrounding both the

---

[97] Jung Chang and Jon Halliday, *Mao: The Unknown Story* (New York: Anchor, 2006), 430.
[98] Karl Marx and Frederick Engels, "The Manifesto of the Communist Party," in *Karl Marx and Frederick Engels: Selected Works* (Moscow: Foreign Languages Publishing House, 1955), vol. I, 34.

means of production and the opposing classes that struggle for them. He had a vision of the future as the end of exploitation—for him, the defining event of all human history and the sole moral good. Thus, like his contemporary descendants, Marx had his own brand of teleology: History is moving toward the future and has a purposeful end.

For Marx, two critical intellectual shifts had to occur as necessary advancements in the pattern of progression he claims. Here we find a clue as to what has displaced our broader notion of origins:

> (1) Philosophy ceased to be a matter of understanding the world and became instead a matter of participating in the progress of history.

As Marx puts it, "The philosophers have only interpreted the world in various ways; the point, however, is to change it."[99] As a thinking person, the socialist man is a revolutionary for whom changing the world is the preeminent concern. A tenet in communist ideology is that all history is concerned with the struggle for power between the exploited and the exploiter; all culture reflects that struggle. The purposeful end of this struggle is socialist society, also called communism. History's chief "actors" are the classes by which Marx identifies everyone and who are insuperably divided from one another. The only way to end class struggle is through the combination of history's force and violent revolution. The shift to

---

[99] Karl Marx, "Theses on Feuerbach," (1845) in *Karl Marx and Frederick Engels: Selected Works* (Moscow: Foreign Language Publishing House, 1955), vol. II, 404.

action helps make sense of the disregard for truth, goodness, and beauty; reality is not in any sense beyond us, it is within us and in our handiwork only. The defining divisions between humans and the violence requisite to completing history should make it obvious that the impulse to change is hardly neutral.

> (2) Religion ceased to be the human response to God's presence and was reinterpreted as the projection of the best of human traits onto a fiction called God.

Marx's close associate, Friederich Engels, declares, "Nothing exists outside nature and man, and the higher beings our religious fantasies have created are only the fantastic reflection of our own essence."[100]

It should be clear that Marxian ideology narrows the socialist man's thoughts on the origins of our existence by transforming philosophy and religion; and, by religion, Marx and Engels mean chiefly Christianity. Marx goes one step further when he prohibits certain questions:

> When you ask about the creation of nature and man, you are abstracting . . . from nature and man. You postulate them as non-existent . . . Give up your abstraction and at the same time you abandon your question."[101]

---

[100] Engels, "Ludwig Feuerbach and the End of Classical German Philosophy" (1886), in *Karl Marx and Frederick Engels: Selected Works* (Moscow: Foreign Language Publishing House, 1955), Vol. II, 366-367.

[101] Karl Marx, *Economic and Philosophic Manuscripts of 1844*, 112.

The loss could hardly be more consequential. This is a direct prohibition on questions concerning ultimate origins. It means both the removal of the transcendent foundations of philosophy and revelation and their displacement as historical sources of meaning and purpose. That shift is not just the removal of two historical features. It is more than the displacement of sources on the scale of the arts or science. To remove philosophy and revelation from our observation and understanding is to lose the two chief normative sources of authority in the West, the standards by which humans discover and know who they are and how they ought to live. Further still, such a shift breaks the unity of our existence; for, without our historical origins, the past is not the past in its fullness and is not, therefore, the foundation for the present and the future.

To state this from another angle, Marxian history is founded on a definitive division: The *we* of history becomes opposing classes, and our existence over time is reduced to the ongoing struggle between classes until the future when exploitation presumably ends. In the present, that future completion of history provides the sole impetus for thought and action. While there is a kind of unity to this history in that all history is the history of class struggle, unity among humans is dealt a fatal blow. In the present we are divided along lines of class and, in the more recent iteration, along lines of gender and race as well. In the future, that division is not to be overcome by the achievement of genuine unity but, rather, by uniformity as the oppressed overcome the oppressors in a final and complete seizure of power.

If, as Marx and his intellectual descendents insist, humans are divided in a definitive way by categories (class, gender, race), then there is little or no common good we presently share and no significantly shared condition that warrants common sympathy, not in the sense of having affinity and shared responsibility for one another. By contrast, from the liberal approach to history, we can recognize differences and unity at the same time. Recall the two figures in Heaney's story: They are Catholic and Protestant. At the same time, they are both Christian, workers, Irish, and, most commonly, human; and each one is facing the threat of violence. Their solidarity is an expression and vision of unity. In the American case, recall the vision of Martin Luther King, Jr., in his "I Have a Dream" speech. There, the American founding would have its further fulfillment when our society finally measures someone by a person's character, not by the color of the person's skin. Our practice of self-governance would be ordered by the common dignity we hold to be noble and worthy, a development initially made possible by principles and laws laid at the founding, then fought for and augmented over the course of our history. America's unity would be formed chiefly by the recognition and protection of personhood in each other.

In the fragmentary approach to history, our differences are underscored, given increased autonomy, and empowered. In that framework, we do not discover who we are in other persons, for persons are reduced to their class, race or gender, no one of which can entirely encompass personhood. The implication is similar concerning our responsibility for one another. Others are not recognized as persons who warrant sacrifice, but mainly or merely as members of one group or the other along the historical divide. Hence, in the fragmentary approach, what defines us is the struggle for power, each group against the other, not mutual personhood and responsibility.

XII. Origins Within and Beyond Ourselves

A culture is the collective practice which renews our visions and extends our sympathies into all the corners of the heart. It is the ongoing record of the life of feeling, which offers to every new generation the examples, images, and words that teach it what to feel.

—Roger Scruton

It should be clear now why the fragmentary approach to history prohibits questions concerning origins. It is precisely because it cannot abide answers that might interrupt the closed system of thought concerning history or deter the will to change the world. By contrast, a liberal approach to history never prohibits questions concerning our origins. Liberal history is always directed toward the most complete picture and open to the acceptance of historical truth wherever it might be found. The liberal approach preserves the primacy of understanding historical change over seeking historical change.

Answering Questions Marx Forbids

There is no reason to accept that history is mainly about exploitation nor that we cannot recognize our common humanity over the distance that lies between the past and today.

All we need do is observe the past at the origins whose consideration is prohibited by the fragmentary mind. If we conduct that observation, what do we find? We find that the West was founded in large measure on two great loves: the love of wisdom, on the one hand, and the love of God and neighbor, on the other. In turn, we find that those loves are expressed in a myriad of ways throughout Western history all the way down to our own time.

This turn to origins is not an arbitrary preference. It is part and parcel of history as a field of study. Turning to the relevant origins simply means observing the birth of philosophy in ancient Greece and revelation in ancient Israel and each as a historical source of our existence as a civilization. Consideration of historical origins is entirely one with consideration of historical facts. For those of us who teach ancient history, it would not do to omit the historical figures central to the emergence of philosophy—Socrates, Plato, and Aristotle, for instance, nor, for another example, the structure of the Temple in Jerusalem, the content of the Torah or the Beatitudes, and the persons of David, Jesus, and Paul, all of whom are at the heart of the emergence of revelation. Each set of facts is integral to the historical study of the two respective societies, ancient Greece and Israel. Each of the two societal histories is integral to the study of the West.

Nor is the turn to origins strictly a matter of religious conviction. True, some questions concerning origins ask us to consider the origin of the world itself. In other words, they are questions concerning creation and as such are not properly historical. At the same time, there is no denying that as a matter of historical observation, philosophy and revelation, which, each in distinctive ways consider the ultimate origins of reality, are direct historical wellsprings of Western civilization. To ignore them is akin to writing a biography without considering the subject's parents or birthplace. To see them for what they are, their emergence as events, and as the unique events that provide us with origins is to satisfy the first liberal rationale for doing history: to observe the past as different. To trace subsequent changes by which philosophy, as it was born in ancient Athens, and revelation, as it emerged chiefly in its Christian expression, formed the world we inhabit is to satisfy the second liberal rationale. To recognize residues of antiquity around us is to meet the third.

Philosophy

In one respect, the emergence of philosophy was one event in a broader set of events called the "discovery of the mind," which began with Homer, progressed through Greece's highest cultural advancements, and culminated in the unveiling of intellect.[102] Homer was the beginning of Western letters, which includes philosophical works. Greek philosophy, in turn, was the principal beginning of formal learning in the West and of Western science, both in its ancient and modern meanings—in other words, the permanent foundation for any systematically organized branch of knowledge.[103]

---

[102] Bruno Snell, *The Discovery of the Mind*, iii.
[103] Bruno Snell, *The Discovery of the Mind*, 226-245.

In another respect, philosophy offered a way of life and a great exemplar of that way in the figure of Socrates, the consummate teacher. His method of teaching afforded his students freedom to seek and discover the truth and to answer for themselves the questions they should ask. Socrates sought the good of everyone who would engage him in discussion; that was his reason for teaching—to improve his interlocutors' souls, to help them choose and live well and freely according to what is true and good. He sought neither power nor wealth; he never left his city except to defend her on the battlefield; and, as a matter of loyalty to Athens and as an example for his friends, Socrates submitted to the laws of Athens, even though it meant accepting an unjust conviction and death. Socrates resisted all forms of domination, personal or public. As such, Socrates is the model for anyone in the West dedicated to the love of learning and for any teacher dedicated to the love of students. In improving his interlocutors, he is a model for anyone devoted to the common good as well, since someone who is truly better, is, at the same time, in a better position to improve the broader society.

The birth of philosophy emerged within the wake of the decimation of Athenian culture. Athens had recently lost a protracted and costly war with Sparta. Once the greatest society in all of Greece and, at the time, in all the world, Athens devolved further from devastating military defeat to tyranny, a fall that was followed by an anemic attempt at democratic revival. Their woes deepened as Athens fell prey to the toxic influences of sophistry. In sum, society had largely become an arena of power struggles, education mainly a means to acquire power.

Socrates is not understandable as part of the prevailing Athenian corruption but as a response to it. His response is best understood as an affirmation of the humanity of his fellow Athenians and their rich cultural inheritance, a reminder of what ends ought to govern life, and a proof of freedom as generosity. He offered Athens a way out of its decline, a way up from the city's corruption. In Socrates we have a teacher of exceptional sympathy, for he knew, from the inside out, life lived in a *polis* struggling between order and disorder, the difficulty of attaining the truth under the pall of the prevailing disorder, and the stakes for his life and for his city's of living truthfully. Socrates was a historical figure responding in the context of a set of events shaping the historical city of Athens.

His student, Plato, and Plato's student, Aristotle, founded communities of learners—the Academy and the Lyceum, respectively, which were later embraced in the West as lasting models for various forms of academies: universities, colleges, schools, institutes, and any mission dedicated to learning and discovery and driven by their chief purpose—understanding reality. No civilization in history has ever developed a comparable culture of learning, nor has any produced a comparable body of knowledge and invention as has the West. Nor has any offered humankind comparable habits of open-mindedness and self-criticism, understood as the individual and social habits of distinguishing between the stronger and weaker arguments, better and worse choices, and truer and less true ways of organizing society.[104] This does not mean that the West is without real, egregious failings. However, it does mean that the West developed a body of wisdom that has always enabled us to articulate what we ought to do. Just think of the formative chain of events that link ancient Greek philosophy, the medieval thinkers Augustine and Aquinas, and Martin Luther King, Jr., who wrote from his jail cell in Birmingham and evaluated contemporary American law in light of natural law theory from centuries ago.[105]

Christianity

Through an extensive set of events, Hellenic thought eventually converged with the Christian faith. Under the impulse of Latin Christianity, the West, rooted in ancient Greece, emerged in full. Pointing out that set of events is not an apology for the Christian faith. It is merely an attempt to clarify the connection between Christianity and the West as a historical matter and as a connection between origins and culture. The connection is not dependent on religious belief but on historical observation.

What, in fact, is that connection? Among its most important contributions, Christianity gave us the concept of personhood

[104] John Heath, "More Quarreling in the Muses' Birdcage," in *The Bonfire of the Humanities*, 83.

[105] Martin Luther King, Jr., "Letter from Birmingham Jail," April 16, 1963, in Edward P.J. Corbette and Robert J. Connors, *Classical Rhetoric for the Modern Student*, Fourth Edition (New York: Oxford Press, 1999) 301-319.

at the heart of Western culture. Each of the following features of the West, for example, has significant origins in the Christian vision of personhood:

(1) Universal human dignity
(2) Commitment to the poor
(3) Limited government

That each person is dignified, bears inexhaustible value, and warrants full consideration, including legal protection, is a conviction largely born from the Christian Gospel. For one thing, the belief took hold in the West that God had not only created the human person in his own image, he had become a human. Nothing else in history has so elevated human dignity. In other words, prior to legislators, jurists, and founders promulgating protections that ought to be accorded each individual, a broad cultural ground was already laid by Christianity. Beyond the establishment of universal rights, the struggle to improve life for specific groups of persons has been fueled by the Christian imagination. For example, a Gospel image of the human person was central to the abolition movement, first in America, then in Britain. Subsequently, it was central in the Social Gospel, Civil Rights, and pro-life movements in America. It influenced the Christian Democrats who led Germany's political, legal, and economic recovery after World War II. And it provided a foundation to Poland's Solidarity Movement and to the reconciliation efforts in post-apartheid South Africa. In other words, all of those modern commitments had ancient Christian personalist roots.

Hand in hand with the belief in universal human dignity was the special place Christianity gave to the poor. In Greek and Roman antiquity, the poor as such were not considered a matter of responsibility. True, as a matter of avoiding instability, not so much because of poverty, all citizens could rightly claim a share of public distributions of corn or money. A widow or orphaned children might warrant provision from the state because the man of the family had fallen in service to the *polis* or empire. However, the poor as such had no special value.[106] The belief that Christ had come to liberate the poor, and that he identified with them, elevated their dignity and heightened society's responsibility for them; nowhere in history had the poor been so valued because they were poor.[107] Rome would convert in no small measure under the influence of Christian service to the Roman poor.[108] Later, the history of hospitals began and developed with Christian charity as did schooling for the poor.[109] So effective were English monasteries in tending to the poor that, in the wake of Henry VIII's decimation of them, Elizabeth I was forced to establish England's first poverty laws. So integral to German culture were Catholic charities that Bismarck, in his statist vision, found it necessary to engage in the *Kulturkampf* against the Church.

Then, there is the foundation of limited government. It may be hard for us to imagine a polity that assumes authority over

---

[106] Michel Riquet, S. J., *Christian Charity in Action* (London: Hawthorn, 1962), 12-13.
[107] Riquet, *Christian Charity in Action*, 21-46.
[108] Jaroslav Pelikan, *The Excellent Empire: The Fall of Rome and the Triumph of the Church* (San Francisco: Harper & Row, 1987), 19.
[109] Riquet, *Christian Charity in Action*, 106-135.

every human good where we do not identify that polity as authoritarian, but in the ancient world, the polis assumed that role. Among other things, this is why Aristotle calls political science the master science since every important human matter falls under the political realm.[110] The idea of a limited state—in the sense that there were goods that the state could not foster on its own and, correspondingly, had no rightful authority over—only developed in Western culture, and only then under the influence of Christian thought. Christianity introduced into the West the idea of another realm to which humans give their allegiance: the Kingdom of God. Although they converge on many points, the temporal and sacred orders ultimately part along lines of distinctive church and state responsibilities, not as a matter of power but as a matter of the freedom of persons to believe, to practice their faith, and to follow their consciences. In America, one enormously important expression of those lines is this: It is not just that there are distinct and protected realms of authority; it is that religious liberty is the first right whose protection Americans can claim among those identified in the Bill of Rights.

There is no history of our society without consideration of such features as individual dignity, care for the poor, and limited government. In other words, they are ingrained in how we understand ourselves; and as a matter of historical fact, they are in significant ways rooted in religious experience, specifically Christian faith. Nor is the history of our society without attention to the culture of learning, and there is no denying that the roots of the Western and American

[110] Aristotle, *Nicomachean Ethics*, I.2.1094a.

academy lie in the advent of philosophy in ancient Greece. Given these features of Western history, we have to conclude that one cannot reconstruct our past in its context, trace the changes that informed our world, or recognize the past's residues among us without those origins restored to historical thinking. To follow Marx's prohibition on questions of origins is not to free oneself. Rather, to follow that prohibition is to embrace a reduction of history as a field of study and, therefore, to concede a loss of intellectual freedom.

XIII. Between Disorder and Order

[T]he civilizational crisis of which everyone so readily speaks, does not by any means have to be born as an inevitable fate... No one is obliged to take part in the spiritual crises of society; on the contrary, everyone is obliged to avoid the folly and live his life in order.

—Eric Voegelin

The liberal restoration of origins to historical thinking is true to the field of history. It is true for two principal reasons. For one thing, without the inclusion of origins, historical understanding is incomplete. For another, the recovery of the great loves born at the beginnings of Western civilization restores the ethical foundations for measuring what society ought to do. There is no getting around the responsibility society has for preserving, governing, and improving the order of life lived together. However, the action required of society must rest on understanding first, and understanding must be as complete as possible, not willfully incomplete as it is when subjected to prohibitions on what may be asked and observed.

As it is, there seems to be a common preference for something higher in every history. The historian's habitual selectivity consistently reflects the primacy of what stands out, what is extraordinary. Even the fragmentary historian focuses on events that are ultimately related to some good above those events, a purpose that transcends exploitation. Even in the fragmentary vision, the inference is clearly and rightly that oppression is immoral; and that must mean that freedom from oppression in some form or another is the good toward which change must be directed, its teleological purpose.

The Threat of Disorder

We call existence lived out according to higher goods, order. Genuine higher goods include, for instance, the ideals articulated in the Declaration of Independence and the Constitution's Preamble. We call the opponent to order, disorder. The two form the dramatic tension of history. Among events, society's movement is at times toward order, at other times toward disorder.

On one level, order is simply the identifiable existence of a society: for example, America or the West with their recognizable features. In regard to existence, the chief threat that disorder poses lies in civil or international war. Those threats and a society's response to them are the chief reasons war occupies so much of our historical study and imagination.

Order also has to do with the evaluative movement of a society or civilization. The chief threat that disorder poses in this case is spiritual and moral: the rise of tyranny, the collapse of trust, the dissolution of institutions of meaning, and, yes, exploitation. These sorts of events are dangers from within a society. The rise of Nazism, for example, was a response to spiritual and moral decay that prevailed in Germany in the wake of World War I, an aggressive ideology built on a distorted pseudo-religion, with Hitler as a false messiah, and a willful reduction of whole categories of human beings to less than human, expressed most darkly in the Holocaust.[111] In turn, the false spiritual and moral outbreaks in the Nazi regime turned Germany to embrace invasion, conquest, and world war.

Order and the Good

Each event selected by the historian and captured within a narrative history is understandable in terms of order. This is true even if an account focuses on disorder. We measure segregation, for example, by integration, not vice versa. We do not dismiss the value of integration because segregation once prevailed. Rather, we weigh the movement toward what is better—integration—as a move toward order. Segregation laws were unjust, their elimination just. Integration advances the good of individuals and the common good; the other diminishes either kind of good.

Either an account of disorder infers its opposite as the standard by which we measure it or it makes no sense as an account of something lacking. In other words, there is no coherent identification of evil without a corresponding recognition of the good that opposes it. Again, even the

[111] See Stefan Zweig, *The World of Yesterday: An Autobiography* (Lincoln: University of Nebraska, 1964), and James M. Rhodes, *The Hitler Movement: A Modern Millenarian Revolution* (Stanford: Hoover Institution Press, 1980).

critique of America as fundamentally a land of exploitation rests ultimately on a proposed good, the end and absence of exploitation, which is the order by which the fragmentary account measures the current and past disorder.

To use a medical analogy, we measure disorder and the recovery from it as we would an unhealthy heart and its healing. The standard of an unhealthy heart is the healthy one. The standard for disorder is the well-ordered state of things.

Self-criticism and Order

Diagnosing social disorder is not a matter of following majority opinion or any prevailing power. It is a matter of self-criticism, a discipline born at the foundations of the West. From Socrates on, the habit of carefully examining what shapes society was developed as a matter of greatest importance. This self-criticism has been an important element in the development of our culture.[112] It is an expression of an endeavor to live according to what is true, to order our lives by what is best, and to give of ourselves to others with their good rightly identified. Truth, self-governance, and generosity are the chief expressions of genuine human freedom and the framework by which order is measured and disorder diagnosed.

As a matter of freedom at every level of our existence, the West has been a culture that thrives on making right distinctions: opinion from knowledge, authority from tyranny,

---

[112] Kagan, Ozment, and Turner, *The Western Heritage*, xxvii; John Heath, "Socrates Redux," in *Bonfire of the Humanities*, 39.

charity from justice, Caesar from God. When distinctions fail and when their corresponding limits on human freedom are forgotten, unjust wars break out; fanatics lop off the heads of sacred statuary and burn their rivals at the stake; whole categories of people are declared non-persons and removed from the protection of law. Such failure is largely a matter of forgetfulness, a failure to maintain an integrity between memory, understanding, and love. When, by contrast, we maintain true distinctions, remember our bearings, and preserve the integrity that inheres in true memory, our society's movement in time becomes a matter of right order and the cultivation of genuine freedom.

We have witnessed in American history that movement back and forth between failure and improvement. In the 1960s, Martin Luther King, Jr., saw that we had from our beginning the resources by which to measure our failure and to improve the order of our society. Through a compelling historical vision, he recounted those resources for the nation and led the way to bring them to bear for improved freedom and greater equality. He invoked the founding principles and Lincoln's political vision as he did in his "I Have a Dream" speech. He built his case on the natural law, as is evident in his "Letter from the Birmingham Jail,"[113] where he encouraged his readers to weigh modern segregation laws as invalid under the analysis of law provided by the medieval writers, Augustine and Aquinas. Reaching even further back in history, King

---

[113] Martin Luther King, Jr., "Letter from Birmingham Jail," in *Classical Rhetoric for the Modern Student*, 301-319.

presented a biblical image of our shared humanity in his speeches and sermons.[114]

None of those sources were of his own creation; they were from beyond him. He remembered them as good and as sources of truth, permitted them to order and inform his reading of America, and allowed them to shape his compelling charge to Americans—to live up to our origins. Remarkably, he did not narrow America to the slave trade, the compromise on slavery at the founding, slavery's growth, Jim Crow laws, lynchings, and a century of segregation. Generously and honestly he confronted the worst of our racial record and measured it by the best of America and the West. He did not dismiss our existence; he affirmed it while never flagging from identifying the country's failings.

King's response to American history is a reminder that the cultivation of genuine order is a response to what has been discovered and revealed about our humanity in the historical condition we all share. In that light, disorder is understandable as the consequence of turning away from the sources that illuminate our condition, a response that closes the mind and reduces the person. That false response turns out to be the necessary condition for relegating whole categories of experience to fiction and whole categories of persons to a status less than persons.

---

[114] Martin Luther King, Jr., *Martin Luther King, Jr. Companion: Quotations from the Speeches, Essays, and Books of Martin Luther King, Jr.*, ed. Coretta Scott King (New York: St. Martin's Press, 1993), 14, 25, 27, 32, 51-54.

XIV. The Future Remembered

That "we live forward but we can only think backward" is true not only of the present (which is always an illusion) but of our entire view of the future, for even when we think of the future we do this by remembering it.

—John Lukacs

History is a matter of the past, and our memory of the past is a source of meaning and purpose for our lives in the present. What, then, if anything, does history have to do with the future?

History and Hope

History as a way of interpreting our existence is completed by hope. On one level of human experience, hope is an expectation of a better future for one of three possible reasons: an improvement of the way things are, a continuation of what we cherish and whose longevity we welcome, or a good completion of events in the future. To say that the future is better is to acknowledge the inherent evaluation of things from and toward which hope directs us. To hope for an end to exploitation or for the expansion of freedom, for example, implies that freedom is a good; to hope for an end to injustice implies that justice, its remedy, is a good.

Hope is at once expectant and evaluative. We see that dual expression in Lincoln, for example, in his vision for popular self-governance as in "government of the people, by the people, for the people"; in his estimation of America as the "last best hope" under that same vision of self-governance; and in his call for national reconciliation as America anticipated the end of the Civil War. Millions of immigrants, for another example, have placed their trust in America for second chances and better lives. For a third, King captivated the nation with his dream of a more just and equal America by ending segregation.

In each of those three cases, the future was a matter of hope:

> (1) That we will fulfill our national promise by victory, by reuniting under charity, and by self-governance
> (2) That the limitations of our individual lives and of our ancestral homes would give way to the expansive opportunities and freedom America affords us
> (3) That we would recover our bearings against the culture of segregation and improve and unite America in ways consistent with what is best in our past

In each case, what we hoped for was something good. Each player—Lincoln, the immigrant, and King—longed for something better. In every case, improvement meant the fulfillment of some good that was already part of our existence as a society.

To hope for a better future is one way to think historically, to think of society's movement, its change. Historical movement is of two kinds: change either in time, as in from the past forward, or in the quality of our existence, as in better or worse. In American history, our existence moves chronologically between the founding and the future. It also moves between disorder and order or between order and disorder. In the case we have been examining, it moves between slavery and freedom, civil war and reconciliation, and segregation and integration. In each change, a better future is not inevitable. Human freedom is always a factor, and order can devolve to disorder. Still, a better future is the object of hope.

Since hope is founded on some preexisting good, and since past changes have not always been for the good, rather than identifying change as the object of hope, it is better to say that improvement is its principal object. Change in history is a given, neither inherently good nor, therefore, precisely the goal we seek. Improving the order of society is the primary goal, built as it is on what is already good and, by virtue of its inherent goodness, providing a lasting object for our hope.

For most of America's history, hope has been central to the public mind. Americans have generally been confident that their foundations were built with true principles and genuine wisdom so that while America has sometimes failed, even egregiously so, Americans have believed in their ability to reorganize around foundational sources and work toward the fulfillment of America's promise. That makes sense of Lincoln's call for reconciliation between the North and South as one nation and of King's dream for a more just America.

The good sought under Lincoln and King's leadership was forged at the founding, gathered as the public's memory and brought forward as an occasion for hope. The call for reconciliation did not ignore the failings of slavery and civil war, nor did the Civil Rights movement glibly forget the century of segregation that followed two-and-a-half centuries of slavery. Rather, in each set of events, because the habits of thinking prevailed by which history was understood in terms of unity and purpose, public memory collected the freedom to transcend those failings and proceeded to cultivate the good, individual and common.

Unlike the fragmentary focus on exploitation, this way of historical thinking is more sympathetic to the human condition. It allows for "malice toward none, [and] charity for all," even between recent enemies; it frees us to embrace a vision of our society, once marked by slavery and then by segregation, where now no one is "judged by the color of their skin but by the content of their character." Neither allowance could hold fast under the narrower lens through which our existence is understood as the history of exploitation and our divided places in that history by class, race, or gender.

Continuity and Hope

In the liberal approach to history, memory and hope are partners. For one thing, they share timelessness as a feature. We remember events that are no longer; and through hope, we are drawn to a better future that does not yet exist in time.

For another, they share goodness as their foundation. The existence of society is the foundational good for all other goods in our society. Our culture is an inheritance, a gift from those who preceded us and ours to bequeath. In turn, the future is better as the continuation of what we have (more of what is good), as an improvement that might develop in the state of things, or as the good completion of past but developing events. Among those three, improvement provides the main draw to hope: a better society, renewal, the promise of the past finally fulfilled—all these are examples of the improvement toward which hope is directed.

Finally, memory informs and shapes our hope regarding others yet to be born. Despite the fact that hope is directed to a future that is not observable, history makes sense of our expectation of and sympathy toward those yet to be born by situating us in the generational changes by which we are connected across time and by revealing the sympathy our forebears had for us. Through observation of the past, we recall that people there not only made our existence as a society possible, they anticipated us. In other words, they were aware of their affinity for us and ours for them and acted with us in mind, as in the founders' constitutional intent to "secure the Blessings of Liberty to ourselves and our Posterity" and as in the sacrifice made for us at Gettysburg in 1863 and Normandy in 1944. This foundation to who we are frees us to think of the future in similar terms. It is a revelation that we meant something to our forebears. In turn, it is one measure of who we are that they mean the world to us. It becomes another that we are invested in our posterity. In other words, by discovering that those who preceded us transcended themselves in expectation of us, history teaches us to transcend ourselves in expectation of those yet to arrive.

The discovery that those who came before us had us in mind and bore us in their sympathy may, understandably, be difficult to accept, given the historical inconsistency that marks the relationship between principles and actions. That inconsistency is a painful reality in America's past and a source of troubling residues today.

Still, the public purpose of liberty for all, articulated in the American founding, is not a lie, as it is construed by some; rather, it is at once true and an end to be achieved as a matter of improving the order of society. Our ongoing quest to secure freedom for every member of our society is made possible by the foundation established nearly two-and-a-half centuries ago and is punctuated in our history by events that advanced and strengthened our efforts. That first foundation is what Lincoln had in mind when he acknowledged that the blood of all those tens of thousands of soldiers who died at Gettysburg laid a second foundation for "a new birth of freedom." The fallen made that freedom possible by a gift of their lives, "the last full measure of their devotion," to those who would live beyond them. A century later, when King invoked the founding, he did not treat it as a pack of lies but as the promise that Lincoln affirmed, the devotion to freedom exhibited on the battlefield of Gettysburg, and the promise for freedom that all of us could embrace as our common purpose. If the founding is a lie, then the ground at Gettysburg is not sacred nor is the freedom made possible by the sacrifice of the soldiers' lives. If the founding is a lie, then King's invocation of the founding as a source of direction for the Civil Rights movement and the country holds no moral authority. Finally, if the founding is a lie, then the relationship King saw between the natural law teaching of Augustine and Aquinas, the principles of the founding, and the moral authority of civil disobedience would be incoherent. Remember, however, the only way the fragmentary approach to history construes the founding as a lie is by taking it out of its full context, by reducing our history to exploitative events, and by emptying reality of goodness with the exception of a yet to be fulfilled future good. Restore the founding to its historical context, observe the full range of events in our history, and recognize the intrinsic goodness in reality that grounds and measures any improvement in genuine freedom, and the founding's ideals are understandable as true and as formative for our existence across the past, present, and future.

How we understand our freedom is directly formed by how we understand our unity over time. What we understand to be true, how we govern our lives by what is lasting and highest and by what sacrifices we rightly make, all rest on the continuity of our existence. Without that continuity, there is no promise to be fulfilled; the past would not penetrate to the meaning of our existence nor give direction to our society's action in the present. Without unity across generations, there is no security of blessings for our posterity, for neither would we inherit society as rightly ours nor rightly bequeath it out of a natural and binding commitment to future generations.

The unity of our existence is evidenced on the inside of history; it is revealed in the details, context, and enduring force of past events. Inside of historical existence is where we observe the past, live in its memory, and hope for the future. As historical creatures, we live out our lives in between two defining acts of giving. First, we have received our place in the world from those who came before us. Now, we preserve, improve, and pass on that gift to others. In between those two events, history, as a formal study and as the common habit of public memory, is a necessary way of thinking. By observing the past, we learn about ourselves as givers of life. By observing us through their own expressions of history, those who follow us will learn the same thing about themselves. Our response in either direction—toward the past in observation and memory or toward the future in hope—is sustained by our sympathy for our shared condition, reliant as we are on each other, each of us responsible for the other, and all of us longing for life yet unseen.

Appendix: A Baker's Dozen on History

Sometimes it is helpful to have a summary resource at your fingertips. With that in mind, here are thirteen features of history to keep close by:

1. Past events, though familiar, are unrepeatable.

2. Some events erupt into the ordinary flow of time and become enduring objects of history.

3. Through history, we observe the past because it is different and because it informs the present.

4. Through memory, we receive the past and recognize our condition sympathetically.

5. Observation and memory together form our understanding of the past.

6. Observation extends to all formative events and to the fullest context of each.

7. Only people have history.

8. History is not an agent that moves or judges past events; even ages do not determine our existence but are merely descriptive.

9. As a concept of unity, history grasps the movement, chronological and qualitative, of the whole of our existence in time.

10. As a genre, history is narrative.

11. History is meaningful, purposeful, and expressive of who and why we are.

12. Human existence originates from within and from beyond ourselves.

13. The future is open; and because of the good we inherit from the past and now cultivate for ourselves and for our posterity, the future is an occasion for hope.

Acknowledgements

To my Cana Academy colleagues—Helen, Jeannette, Mary Frances, and Michaela in our Virginia headquarters and Andrew out in Texas—I am truly grateful for your intelligent guidance in the completion of this book. Your skillful editing improved the content of the text, your encouragement the spirit of its author.